KEYS TO AVOIDING PROBATE AND REDUCING ESTATE TAXES

by

Adriane G. Berg, Esq.

Estates and Trusts Counsel
Friedland Fishbein Laifer and Robbins
New York City

BARRON'S

All inquiries should be addressed to:
Barron's Educational Series, Inc.
250 Wireless Boulevard
Hauppauge, New York 11788

Library of Congress Catalog Card Number 91-18076

International Standard Book No. 0-8120-4668-4

Library of Congress Cataloging in Publication Data

Berg, Adriane G. (Adriane Gilda),
    Keys to avoiding probate and reducing estate taxes / Adriane G. Berg
        p. cm. — (Barron's business keys)
    Includes index.
    ISBN 0-8120-4668-4
    1. Probate law and practice—United States—Popular works.
Inheritance and transfer tax—Law and legislation—United States—Popular
works. I. Title. II. Series.
KF765.Z9B47 1991
343.7305'32—dc20   91-18076
    [347.303532]   CIP

PRINTED IN THE UNITED STATES OF AMERICA
   45   5500   9876543

Portions of Keys 21, 22, 33, and 47 are reprinted from *Moneythink* by
Adriane G. Berg (Pilgrim Press, 1981).

CONTENTS

INTRODUCTION

Today, people who never dreamed they would need an estate plan are anxious to learn about probate, taxes, and wealthbuilding. If you are one of them, it's probably because you have more assets than you ever expected and they are in greater danger from taxes, health care costs, and your own potential for a long life than you ever anticipated. You may also be a grandparent or parent intent on protecting family assets for future generations.

Chances are you have heard or lived through horror stories about depleted and impoverished fortunes and hard-working, middle-class people who could not fulfill their dreams because of bad planning or unscrupulous professional help.

It's a more complicated world than ever before. Yet, by grasping certain easy principles, explained in plain English, you can avoid a multitude of costly and sometimes devastating mistakes.

I am happy that I can help. For twenty years I have been a lawyer, and for a dozen years a financial and insurance professional. Today I am counsel to the trusts and estates law firm of Friedland Fishbein Laifer and Robbins in New York City. I am also a radio and television financial and legal broadcaster and public speaker. I have learned what you need to know, what troubles you, and what confuses you. In the next fifty Keys, I will attempt to correct a lot of misinformation and present valid information that will serve you and your family for years to come. Join me as we unravel the myths and truths of good estate planning.

1

WHAT IS PROBATE?

Many people would like to avoid probate, but very few actually know what probate is. Moreover, they are surprised when one attorney welcomes their business while another lectures them on why they should not avoid probate. The experiences of friends can be confusing too. Some will pay any price to avoid probate; others think it's a foolish, legal fad, a waste of time, thought, and money. So who's right?

Actually, both pros and cons have merit. Whether you should avoid probate or not depends on the comparative costs, your family structure, the type and location of your assets, and your motivation to make life simpler for others at the expense of doing extra work yourself.

Probate is a legal proceeding. It takes place in the state court of the state in which a decedent resided at the time of death. The name of the court varies from state to state. In New York, for example, probate takes place in the surrogates court, but in New Jersey, probate takes place in the chancery court. There's a reason that the language associated with probate sounds so British: most of our laws and rules are derived from old English decisions on inheritance. The primary goal of those early proceedings was to make sure that the wishes of the decedent were carried out to the letter, no matter how much it cost the family (sometimes the whole estate) and no matter how long it took (sometimes years).

Today probate starts with a petition to the court stating who died and when. The petition describes the estate and requests the court to accept the accompanying will as authentic. After the petition is filed, notice must be given in accordance with state law. Requirements vary, but most states require notice by mail with proof of mailing to everyone mentioned in the will, along with the legal next of kin as defined in the statutes of the state.

After notice is complete, the court sets a date to admit the will to probate. Anyone with an interest in the estate can object. Reasons for objecting include: the will is a forgery; the decedent was forced to sign; the decedent was not mentally competent; and the spouse or other potential heir was wrongfully cut out. And these are only a few. In addition, objections are made in public. Anyone can go into a courtroom for an afternoon of observation and entertainment.

If there are no objections, the court will usually admit the will to probate, although the court can object, too. Once the will is admitted to probate, the court issues a letter testamentary. This document appoints the person(s) or entity named in the will as the executor and confers the power to distribute the assets to the heirs as instructed in the will.

When all distributions have been completed to everyone's satisfaction, releases are given to the executor and the estate is closed. There are a lot of places where things can go wrong, take time, or cost money, but it can also go smoothly and serve to protect all parties. In the next Key we discuss some myths about probate that have given it a bad name.

2

THE SIX MYTHS OF PROBATE

Myth 1: *If you avoid probate you save taxes.* False. Probate has nothing whatever to do with taxation. Taxes are based entirely upon the assets in your control when you die. If you avoid probate entirely, you will still be taxed under the same rules and in the same amount that you would be if your estate was probated.

Myth 2: *Probate is handled by the Internal Revenue Service.* False. Probate takes place in the state court in the state of residence at the time of death. These courts were once called widows' and orphans' courts. Today, they are known as chancery or surrogate's courts. "Surrogate" is another word for substitute; the judge in these courts is a substitute for the deceased. If there is any question about what the deceased meant in the will or intended at the time of death, the surrogate (the judge) will decide. Surrogate's court judges act in place of the deceased in carrying out the wishes of that individual.

Myth 3: *If you have no will you will not need probate.* False. If there is no will, the court must appoint an administrator. That requires a member of the family or other interested party going to the probate court to be designated as administrator. One client whose mother had died found $1,000 in a joint account and a few hundred dollars in an individual checking account. There was also a life insurance policy of $2,000. The mother had left no will because the estate was so small. In order to obtain the money in the individual

4

checking account, the client had to go to the local county surrogate's court and apply to be named administrator. Only after being so named could she apply for the tax waivers necessary to withdraw the funds. Her mother certainly had not avoided probate by not having a will.

Myth 4: *Probate takes place in only one state.* False. Residence is the key to probate. In our mobile society people often reside in more than one place. The older couple who keeps a condominium in Florida and a vacation home in Connecticut can have double trouble when it comes to probate. Where do they reside? In determining residence, the court will look to where the deceased voted, kept property, kept bank accounts, worked, and had friends. The residence listed in a will is not binding on the court. Sometimes an ancillary side proceeding is needed to probate a piece of real estate that was owned by the deceased and located in a state other than that of residence.

Myth 5: *While probate is proceeding no money is distributed to the heirs.* False. A good executor (one with a heart and a head) knows the needs of the beneficiaries and makes every effort to distribute funds as probate goes along, particularly if the probate proceeding will take a long period of time.

Myth 6: *If everything is in joint names, probate can be avoided.* False. There are many kinds of joint ownership. Ownership with right of survivorship insures that the survivor will automatically inherit, and this automatic inheritance does avoid probate. Not all joint ownerships, however, have the right of survivorship. In most states, if assets are held jointly with no special provisions regarding survivorship, a "tenancy in common" is created. The deceased's share must be probated.

3

THE PITFALLS OF PROBATE

To help decide whether to expend the effort it takes to avoid probate, it's useful to know where things can go wrong and see how likely it is that problems will arise. Here are the pitfalls:

1. *Cost*—Probate can be expensive. One American Bar Association (ABA) report estimated that attorneys' fees are one-and-a-quarter times statutory executors' fees. Such fees average 5 percent of an estate, making attorneys' fees 6 $\frac{1}{4}$ percent. In most states, attorneys' fees can be reviewed, and in some cases court review is mandatory. In fact, most lawyers charge by the hour rather than by the size of the estate. Either way, probate can cost a lot. If a complication occurs, the cost can be out of proportion to the assets. Even if things go well, just the court costs can be high. Filing fees alone can be as much as $1,000 in the state of New York.

2. *Time*—There is no average period of time for going through probate. First, the lawyer must get all the necessary facts to prepare the petition, including an original will, along with a list of assets and their location and a list of heirs and their location. Then the petition, which can be several pages long, must be prepared and filed with the will. The court clerk won't accept the papers if they don't comply with formal court regulations or if the will doesn't have all the

6

right signatures or other formalities. Sometimes years go by in cases where witnesses cannot be found. Next, the court must have an open calendar date to hear the petition and the judge, lawyer, and executor must all appear on that date or probate is postponed. It can also take quite a while to reach the heirs and others who must, by law, be notified.

Of course, if there is a will contest, the proceeding can last indefinitely. For example, if some children are dissatisfied with their share and claim that the decedent was unduly influenced by a sibling, they may be entitled to a jury trial to decide the case.

3. *Family stress*—Apart from the grief of losing a loved one, going to court is never a pleasure. Even with a simple probate, stress can result from the experience of dealing with the unfamiliar world of our judicial system. But the problem is deeper. Since our system is adversarial, a family dispute is likely to aggravate feelings and keep people apart. Some feuding families never recover from a probate battle.

4. *Double probate*—If the decedent has property in more than one state, there will be a main probate in the state of residence and an ancillary probate in the state where real estate and certain other property is located. This doubles the problems of cost and time already discussed.

In the next Key, you will be asked to answer some questions to help decide whether or not you want to avoid probate.

4

NONPROBATE PRIVACY COMPARED WITH COURT REVIEW

On a separate sheet of paper, respond to the following questions. If you have substantially more "yes" than "no" answers, you are a good candidate to avoid probate.

1. My loved ones are not very competent about money and legal matters. In fact, I usually take care of those things.
2. My affairs are complicated because I have many different types of investments.
3. I have investments, especially real estate, in more than one state.
4. My heirs are scattered all over the place, living in three or more different states.
5. One or more of my heirs lives in a foreign country.
6. We have no trusted family attorney and my heirs would have to find a lawyer to handle the probate.
7. I plan to disown one of my children.
8. I am divorced and I want to keep as much privacy in my affairs as possible.
9. I have business or other reasons that make privacy important to me.
10. I plan to give different amounts of money to my brothers and sisters and I would like to keep the amounts private.

11. I don't mind footing the bill during my lifetime (the cost ranges from $1,000 to $50,000) because it will save my family money when I'm gone.
12. I don't mind that my assets won't have my name on them but will be held in the name of a trust, as long as I have full control over them.
13. I don't mind going through boring legal paperwork with an attorney to save my family time and aggravation when I'm gone.
14. I like the idea that by avoiding probate I can simultaneously work out a system for handling my money if I become incompetent.
15. I have no trouble deciding who my trustees will be and I don't believe I need a court to act as a watchdog over them.
16. I don't believe any of my loved ones need special protection from each other or oversight by a court.
17. I have heard some horror stories about probate from people who are in a similar position, and it would give me comfort to avoid probate.
18. My loved ones have read about avoiding probate and seem to favor it.
19. I plan to retire in the Sunbelt, where probate avoidance is very popular and commonplace.
20. In answering these questions, I believe my spouse feels substantially the same.

How did you do? If you are ready to do the work, spend the money, spare your loved ones, and keep your privacy, by all means avoid probate. If you believe the heirs should handle their own affairs, bear the costs, and take advantage of the watch-dog protection of the courts, by all means make a valid will that will go through probate. Because most of you will opt to avoid probate (or you would not have been interested in this book in the first place), the next Key outlines the problems involved in avoiding probate.

5

THE COST OF AVOIDING PROBATE, MONETARY AND OTHERWISE

You pay a price for everything, including avoiding probate. Here's the downside:

1. *Upfront cost* —While the cost of probate is paid by your estate, the cost of *avoiding* probate is paid by you, and it can be expensive. Attorneys will charge on a time basis and give you an estimate before you begin. Rarely will the process and documents cost less than $1,000, and this is very conservative. A current estimate is $2,500 for planning, tax review, a trust, a side will, a power of attorney, and additional clauses. Geographic location is a big factor in the cost. As with most expenses, you'll pay more in large urban areas. You'll also pay more if you have a complicated estate or if you are indecisive about your wishes and require multiple changes in the documents.

2. *Upfront work* —Avoiding probate is a lot of work for you as well as for your lawyer. You must list all of your assets, make all the usual decisions that you would for a will, and work with your lawyer to change the name on most of your assets to the name of a probate-avoiding trust or other device, depending on the method you select. After your lawyer's job is finished, yours isn't. You must be vigilant in keeping new assets in the proper name for the rest of your life.

10

3. *Finding a lawyer* —Most lawyers, including some very good ones, will not help you avoid probate. Many don't believe in it. Their position is that a smooth probate is more protective of your wishes because it takes place under the eye of the court. This circumstance sometimes means that many inexperienced lawyers who are not trust-and-estate specialists have purchased a computer program and gone into the probate-avoidance business. In a later Key you'll learn how to select a lawyer.

4. *The emotional component* —To avoid probate, your assets must be placed in a name other than your own (although it can be in joint names) or, in some cases, in a beneficiary's name. If you opt for a trust, your assets are owned by the trust even though you control them. Naturally, this is a constant reminder of your mortality and is emotionally contrary to the American preference for proprietary ownership.

5. *It doesn't always work* — Even if you and your lawyer do everything right, if there are truly dissatisfied heirs, they may still bring a lawsuit. With probate, they are invited to object, but even without probate they can wage a legal battle to set aside a trust or joint account if they have the grounds and the grudge.

In case you're having second thoughts, the secrets of preparing a will for an easy probate will be discussed in the next Key.

6

PREPARING A WILL FOR AN EASY PROBATE

The chance of a smooth probate is increased by the following important rules:

1. *Make the will self-proving* —In most states, the court will not require the testimony or affidavits of witnesses if the will is accompanied by an affidavit (made at the time you signed it) from the witnesses saying that they knew you signed the will and understood it. This documentation is enough to satisfy the court that you were not under duress when you made the will. Months and money are saved by avoiding the problems of finding the witnesses at the time of probate or proving that a witness has passed away.

2. *Keep it simple* —In an attempt to control from the grave, some people put complicated provisions and hard-to-follow trust restrictions in their wills. This can tie an estate up in knots. Work with your attorney to create a simple expression of your wishes.

3. *Use legal jargon* —This rule may seem strange, but if you want a smooth probate, your will should use time-honored language, even if archaic, that's understood by a judge. If you don't understand the terminology, have your attorney explain it to you, but leave the legal language in the will.

4. *Introduce your lawyer to your beneficiaries* — An introduction will save time and money and avoid shopping for a probate attorney.

5. *Keep a list of all of your assets where your executor can find it* —Be sure your executor knows what you own, what you paid for it, what you think it's worth, and why. That person should also know where to find stock certificate deeds and any other important papers.

6. *Never keep your papers in a safety deposit box* —In some states, a court order and the presence of a Marshal is required to open the box.

7. *Don't put a big list of personal property in your will* —Jewelry, china, even art can be lost, stolen, or misplaced, delaying the closing of the estate. Unless the property is very valuable, allow the executor to distribute personal property and leave a letter with your intent along with your important papers.

8. *If you plan to disown an heir, say so* —Every state has its own unique clause that effectively disowns an heir. Don't just ignore the issue—use the clause.

9. *Don't make codiciles* —If you decide to change a provision, make a new will. It should cost very little more than a codicile that must also be proved and admitted to probate.

10. *Have a simultaneous death clause* —Be sure your will says what should happen if both you and your heirs die in a common accident. And be sure you name a successor executor so the court doesn't have to appoint one if the need arises.

Of course there are ways to get your assets to your loved ones without wills, trusts courts, or lawyers. In the next few Keys, you'll learn how to do this—and avoid probate as well.

7

AVOIDING PROBATE WITH A LIFE INSURANCE WILL

If you own an asset that designates a beneficiary, that designation supersedes the terms of the will, and the beneficiary will inherit the asset without an executor's signature and therefore without probate. That is the general rule for avoiding probate: merely name a beneficiary of an asset. Not every asset allows for such a designation, but one asset for which it works very well is an insurance policy.

When you apply for any life insurance policy, you are asked to name a beneficiary, a contingent beneficiary, and an owner. You, of course, are the insured, but that just means that yours is the measuring life. The death benefit will be paid upon your demise. But to whom? That depends on what you write in the blank marked "beneficiary." You can designate your spouse, child, or any other person who has an insurable interest in your life.

The definition of insurable interest varies from state to state and from company to company, but parents, siblings, and business partners always qualify. Close friends, lovers, or roommates (as designated beneficiaries) are often questioned by the insurance underwriter. You may be asked to give an explanation of why you want them to benefit at your death. Often such beneficiaries are also co-owners of property with you and can qualify on that basis.

Once you have designated the beneficiary, that person will automatically receive the proceeds of the policy upon your death. There is no need for probate. In fact, if you have a will designating a different person as the beneficiary of your policy, it is the designation on the application, not the designation in the will, that prevails.

If your beneficiary predeceases you, the person you named as the contingent beneficiary will inherit the proceeds. You can do a very thorough job by naming a beneficiary and adding the words "*per stirpes*." This is a Latin legal designation that leaves the proceeds to the named heir, or if he should predecease you, to his heirs. For example, "To my son *per stirpes*" means to my son, but if he is dead, to my grandchildren by him, and if they are gone, to my great-grandchildren.

An insurance policy also allows naming an owner other than yourself, but once you do this, you no longer control the policy. You can't borrow against it, change the beneficiary, or dictate how the dividends will be used. On the other hand, by giving up owner-ship the proceeds are kept out of your estate for estate-tax purposes. If you wish to give up ownership of an existing policy that has cash surrender value, check with your accountant first. You might be subject to a gift tax.

Avoiding probate by designating a beneficiary works with other assets too. In the next Key, we'll address how to do that in pensions and other plans.

8

ASSETS THAT ACCEPT A "DESIGNATION OF BENEFICIARY"

A simple way to avoid probate is to name the beneficiary on the ownership papers of an asset. Naming the beneficiary is called a designation. The beneficiary is the person who will inherit the asset.

A designation of beneficiary is a very powerful method of avoiding probate because the designation supersedes a will. If, for example, you designated your son as the beneficiary of your life insurance policy, but in your will you gave the proceeds to your daughter, your son would inherit the policy proceeds. Remember, if you decide not to avoid probate, make sure that you have not designated a beneficiary on the ownership papers that is contrary to the wishes expressed in the will.

Not every type of asset has ownership papers that allow for a designation of beneficiary. Important ones that do include:

- life insurance policies.

- disability policies.

- annuities.

- IRA (individual retirement accounts).

- pensions of all types, including 401K, 403b, defined benefit, profit sharing, defined contribution, and Keogh plans.

Every time you participate in a pension plan, buy an asset, or make an investment, ask whether you can designate a beneficiary to avoid the probate of an asset.

Sometimes, even though you could avoid probate, there will be reasons you'd rather not designate a beneficiary. Some of these reasons are:

- You have a tax strategy that requires an asset to be paid into a trust or to your estate.

- Your spouse or other beneficiary is elderly and may not be able to handle the asset.

- Your beneficiary is a minor and may not be able to handle an asset.

- Your beneficiary is influenced by another (perhaps in a bad marriage) whom you don't want to benefit.

- Your beneficiary is entitled to government aid that would be lost by direct inheritance.

- Your beneficiary is mentally, emotionally, or physically unable to handle the asset or its proceeds.

- Your distribution is involved (i.e., a fractional share going to each beneficiary or a trust arrangement).

If for any of these or other reasons you do not wish to designate a beneficiary, you may name a trust or your estate as the beneficiary. In the former case, the asset will be paid to the trustee and be distributed in accordance with the provisions of the trust. In the latter case, the asset will be paid over to the executor of your will, or if you have no will, to the administrator of your estate. The distribution will be in accordance with the provisions of the will or, if there is no will, in accordance with state law. Remember, proceeds paid directly to an estate can lose protection against creditors. This will be discussed further in Key 20.

9

HOW TO DESIGNATE A BENEFICIARY

Whether you decide to name a person(s), a trust, or your estate as the beneficiary, it is your job to be sure the designation is correctly made. Don't rely on the insurance agent, the pension planner, your company's personnel and benefits officer, or even your lawyer.

In most cases, you will be asked to designate the beneficiary on the application for the insurance, annuity, or pension plan. It is likely that the subject will never come up again. Once you make the designation, it will stay that way unless you contact the institution handling the asset (the insurance company, the bank, or the custodian) and change the designation. Good intentions are of no value. If you meant to make a change but never did, the asset holder is required to go by the designation and nothing more. A man who was a lawyer and an accountant never changed the beneficiary designation on the life insurance that he had purchased before his marriage. When he died twenty years later leaving a wife and child, his mother received the proceeds.

Don't be intimidated by the tiny space provided for the beneficiary. If necessary, insist on a supplementary page to be made part of the application, allowing room to write.

Be prepared with the words of designation you plan to use. Here are some examples:

- to designate a trust as beneficiary— "John Jones as

18

trustee for the revocable trust of Benjamin Franklin dated July 21, 1776."

- to designate an estate as beneficiary— "The estate of Benjamin Franklin."

- to designate a spouse and children— "to my wife Sarah, and if she shall predecease me to my children equally, or if any should predecease me to their heirs *per stirpes* (down the line of decent)."

- to designate siblings— "To my brother Joseph Jones one-third and to my sister Mary Jones two-thirds or if one shall predecease me, all to the other."

In fact, you can make any designation of beneficiary permitted to be made in a will. The person selling you the asset will probably frown in annoyance. Just explain that this asset is so important that you refuse to give this aspect short shrift. After all, if the money doesn't get to the right person, why buy the asset at all?

Some applications also ask you to name a contingent beneficiary. Use the phrases suggested above and write "see above" in the space marked contingent beneficiary.

10

USING JOINT ACCOUNTS TO AVOID PROBATE

A joint account places legal ownership and control of an asset in the hands of all the parties named as joint owners. Unlike the "designation of ownership" discussed above, creating a joint ownership affects legal title during the lifetime of the asset holder. For example, if Grandma puts her grandchild's name on a bankbook as joint owner, the grandchild owns half the assets immediately. If the child has creditors, they can put a lien on the account. If the grandchild has possession of the passbook, the funds might be withdrawn. Furthermore, while a court might find that Grandma is half owner, a creditor is able to collect on the entire account and each joint owner can withdraw all of the funds.

Because ownership and control is in the legal name of two or more parties, when one dies the asset need not go through probate. Probate is necessary only when an executor is needed to distribute a decedent's assets. No fiduciary is necessary in the case of a joint account. The joint owner(s) merely makes the withdrawal and reinvests the proceeds in the same or another asset.

As you will see in Key 27, this does not mean that the assets escape taxation. On the contrary, the entire value of the asset is counted in the decedent's estate unless the survivors can prove that part of the original funds came from the survivors. Further, when a joint account or other joint ownership is created by placing a second name on an existing asset (Grandma asks the bank to change an account from her name alone to hers and her grandson's), this transfer is a gift and the gift-tax laws apply. See Key 27.

The consequences of joint ownership are often surprising. You must be clear about just what you are doing when you joint-name your assets to avoid probate.

1. If the joint owners are husband and wife, the asset will go without probate to the survivor.
2. If the husband and wife divorce and leave the asset unchanged, most states will still give the entire asset to the survivor.
3. If the joint owners have any relationship other than husband and wife, in most states the asset (including real estate) will go to the survivor only if the words "with right of survivorship" are used after the names.
4. If those words are not used and the owners are not husband and wife, then the ownership is deemed a "tenancy in common."
5. If a joint ownership is a tenancy in common, then upon the death of one owner, one-half of the asset will pass without probate to the heirs of the decedent even if that does not include the surviving joint owner. The other half will remain owned by the survivor. This means that a father and son as joint owners could end up with a son and second wife as joint owners upon the death of the father. Many strange and unexpected combinations have resulted from the use of joint ownership.

To decide if joint ownership is right for you, study the chart on page 22.

Millions of people in this country, especially the elderly, create joint accounts, believing they are saving taxes as well as avoiding probate. They have no idea that their life savings can be taken by the joint owner's

Traits	Right of Survivorship	In Common	Husband & Wife
survivors get all	yes	no	yes
creditors can take	yes	50%	usually
taxed in estate	100%	50%	50%
each can sell, without other's permission	no	yes	no

creditors. If you're still not convinced that joint owner-ship to avoid probate must be properly planned, con-sider the story of the Sad Sisters.

Two sisters, one widowed and one never married, lived as joint tenants in a home. The home was their only asset. They paid the mortgage, made repairs, and cherished the residence for thirty years. All of their siblings died, leaving heirs who were estranged from the sisters.

It was each sister's wish that the survivor inherit the whole house upon the death of the other. But the deed merely read "Sister X and Sister Y." When Sister X died, Sister Y was only a tenant in common. She owned one-half of the house (her share) and one-sixth of the decedent's share. An assortment of nieces and nephews (the estranged relatives) owned the remaining shares. They forced the surviving sister out of the house, a result never intended by either sister.

11

JOINT ACCOUNTS IN THE EVENT OF SIMULTANEOUS DEATH

An often disregarded problem in the use of the joint account is the simultaneous death of the jointly named parties. The same problem will result when custodial and "payable on death accounts" are used (see Keys 12 and 13).

With plane travel, daredevil sports, and natural disasters in mind, along with other events that have contributed to raising the accidental death rate in this country, most states have passed the Uniform Simultaneous Death Act. The provisions of this law specify that when two people die in such a manner that it is not possible to determine who died first, each is presumed to have survived the other for estate distribution purposes.

If a mother and daughter die in a car crash, for example, assets that the daughter would have inherited if she survived the mother will instead be inherited by the mother's next heir in line. The daughter will be presumed to have died first. By a legal fiction, when it comes to determining if the mother inherits from the daughter, the mother will be presumed to have predeceased the daughter. The purpose of this artificial procedure is to save the costs of double probates by avoiding already deceased parties inheriting assets that must then immediately be paid out to their surviving heirs.

While this makes good sense, not every state has adopted the law and laws change, sometimes without notice. Further, the actual effect of a simultaneous death is often not fully understood until distribution is complete.

In the case of a will, the attorney is likely to have worked out a clause that agrees with the testator's wishes. However, in the case of joint ownership or designated beneficiaries, there is usually no thought given to the possibility of simultaneous death.

Several Keys discuss various methods of avoiding probate by mere designation of beneficiary, which you will learn as you go through this book. If it is your practice to travel with your next of kin on many occasions, or if there are other reasons for you to be concerned about joint disasters, you may well find it desirable to consider a probate-avoiding trust. They are described in Key 15.

12

USING IN-TRUST-FOR ACCOUNTS AND PODS TO AVOID PROBATE

Many people, most often grandparents, plan to avoid probate by setting up an "in-trust-for account" called a Totten Trust, with their bank. The title of the account reads "Grandma Jones, in trust for her Grandson Jones." The intent is to keep control over the funds until death when they will automatically be transferred to the beneficiary without probate.

Warning: This procedure frequently creates more problems than it solves. First, if it is a true trust and there is a will, the in-trust-for account supersedes the will, so be sure the two are not in conflict. Second, if the signature card used by the bank permits the depositor (in this case, Grandma) to use the funds at her discretion, the account may not qualify as a true trust under state law. If it does not, the funds will not avoid probate. If there is no will, an administration may be necessary.

Many states have adopted the "New York rule," which qualifies such bank account trusts for probate avoidance even if the depositor keeps control of the money. However, if the beneficiary predeceases the depositor, the money reverts back to full ownership of the depositor. (See Key 11 for the effect of simultaneous death.)

If you have established such accounts, check with your bank to learn the status of these accounts in your state of residence. Above all, be aware that Totten

Trusts do not save any estate or income taxes whatsoever. In fact, since the depositor has kept control over the asset, the tax on income earned by the funds is paid by the depositor. This happens even if the depositor has placed the beneficiary's social security number on the account.

Similarly, the Totten Trust does not protect you in the event of your incompetency. Unless you have executed a durable power of attorney (see Key 23), the funds cannot be administered during your lifetime without a court order. In addition, Totten Trusts are counted as part of your assets in determining whether or not you are eligible for Medicaid and other government programs.

A different caution comes for those designating a minor as a beneficiary. Because minors cannot handle the money, a bank will require that a guardian represent them when the depositor dies. The matter is less difficult if there is an intact marriage, but it can get sticky in the event of divorce. If there are no living guardians, the court will step in and appoint one—in all likelihood, a stranger. There is a further discussion about designating minors as beneficiaries in Key 13.

Obviously, in deciding whether to rely on the Totten Trust, you must weigh the pitfalls of probate and the cost of making a probate that avoids a trust against the relative ease of the Totten Trust. But you must be aware that such accounts afford little opportunity for any real planning.

A less popular but similar procedure is the POD (payable on death) account. Here too, the depositor does not relinquish rights to the funds. The bank or other holder of the funds is merely instructed to pay the named beneficiary in the event of the depositor's death. The same benefits and pitfalls of the Totten Trust apply.

To review:

- Probate is avoided.

- An executor of a will may choose to attack the designation if the will is in conflict.

- In the event that the beneficiary dies first, there is no planning.

- In the event of a simultaneous death, state law applies.

- No taxes are saved.

- There is no protection for the depositor in the event of incompetency.

In short, both of these methods can work to avoid probate, but they can backfire if not carefully considered. They must never be used as a substitute for good planning.

13

USING CUSTODIAL ACCOUNTS TO AVOID PROBATE

Often, the beneficiary of funds is a minor at the time a plan is made to avoid probate. The definition of minor varies from state to state, but most often is defined as a person younger than 18 or 21 years of age. If funds are given outright or placed in a POD or Totten Trust and the depositor dies, a guardian must be appointed to handle the funds. Further, as discussed in Key 12, there are no tax savings.

For this reason, many people set up custodial accounts under the Uniform Gifts To Minors Act, now adopted in every state. It provides for the giving of money, securities, life insurance policies, or annuities to minors.

A custodian must be appointed to manage these funds for the minor. Any adult family member or guardian can act as custodian. If a professional is appointed to manage these gifts for the minor, a fee will be charged. If the gift is of money, life insurance, annuities, or registered securities, the donor of the gift may act as custodian, but if unregistered securities are given, the donor may not be appointed custodian.

The custodian is empowered to manage, hold, and invest the property of the minor. That person may sell or exchange the property and use the proceeds for the minor. The custodian must also keep careful records, register all securities, and establish a bank account for the money. In short, the custodian assumes all fiduciary responsibility for the property.

The minor receives the money upon reaching the age of majority. If the minor dies before reaching majority the funds become part of the heir's gross estate. Once given, the gift is irrevocable and it belongs to the minor. Although the custodian is empowered to control the funds, any taxes due are taxed to the minor, not the custodian. See Key 33 for an explanation of the Kiddie Tax.

Forms for establishing a trust under the Uniform Gifts To Minors Act are available through banks and brokerage firms.

PRO	CON
1. The income from the funds is taxed at the minors rate (best if the child is over 14 because of Kiddie Tax).	1. The gift is irrevocable.
2. Use of money is controlled by the custodian without court intervention until the child is of age.	2. If the donee dies, the funds are taxed in his or her estate.
3. Funds avoid probate.	3. The money becomes the donee's at majority.

14

WHAT IS A TRUST?

In the next several Keys you will read about many different probate and tax savings strategies that involve trusts. Before we begin, let's get an overall picture of a trust.

A trust is a legal device whereby one person (called the grantor) transfers assets (called the corpus) to another person (called the trustee) for the benefit of a third person (called the beneficiary).

Note the word "person" in the definition. This is only to simplify. In practice, a partnership, corporation, or charity (rather than an individual person) can act as trustee, grantor, or beneficiary. Even another trust can act in that capacity.

The main characteristic of a trust is that a third party benefits from the transfer and handling of money by others. In certain types of trusts, like the revocable trust that helps avoid probate, it is usual for the grantor, trustee, and beneficiary to all be the same person. The trust document creates a new legal identity as far as the trust is concerned.

An attorney usually draws up this document by request, with the desired provisions. Most trusts take the place of a will with respect to the assets held in the trust. In fact, a trust supersedes a conflicting provision in a will in relationship to trust assets. That is why the distribution of trust assets must be carefully considered when working with a professional in designing a trust.

Trusts have many characteristics that will be discussed later. Some include:

- revocable vs. irrevocable: The difference is whether or not the trust can be changed or voided after it is made.

- *inter-vivos* or testamentary: Either the trust is made and takes effect during one's lifetime (an *inter-vivos* or living trust) or is part of a will or other trust that does not go into effect until death occurs (a testamentary trust).

- purpose: One trust can serve a single purpose or many, such as substituting for a will and avoiding probate, saving estate taxes, transferring asset management, controlling asset distribution far beyond death, or lowering the income tax effecting an asset's performance. Whatever the purpose, a trust must conform to the requirements of the law in the state where it is made. Unless it severally is contrary to public policy of a different state, it will be recognized there as valid, if valid in the state where it is made.

In the next several Keys, a more complete view of how to use a trust to your benefit will be presented.

15

COMPARING *INTER-VIVOS* TRUSTS WITH TESTAMENTARY TRUSTS

Trusts that are made and take effect during your lifetime are called *inter-vivos* trusts. Trusts made upon your death and mandated in your will are called testamentary trusts. The effects of the two are quite different. Here are the basic definitions of these two kinds of trusts:

- *Inter-vivos* trusts: The Latin literally means "between" (*inter*) and "living persons" (*vivos*). These are trusts that are created during your lifetime. They can be revocable or irrevocable. You may name yourself as trustee. You can specify that the trust will terminate at your death or during your lifetime.

- The assets in an *inter-vivos* trust can "pour over" into a testamentary trust (one that takes effect upon death). As a result the assets will remain in trust even after your death.

- Testamentary trusts: These trusts are created only in a will or in a testamentary substitute for a will (discussed later in this book). They are part of your last wishes and are implemented by a trustee after your demise. If your will is changed, the trust instructions can be revoked or amended.

Inter-vivos (Irrevocable) Trust	Testamentary Trust
takes effect while you are alive	takes effect at your death
saves estate and income taxes	gives no estate or income tax advantage
takes assets permanently out of your ownership and control	assets remain yours during your lifetime
gets its own tax identification	allows long-range tax planning
allows you to see how your assets will be managed	controls the use of money even after death
allows you to designate a beneficiary of the income and a beneficiary of the principal when the income-beneficiary dies	allows you to designate a beneficiary of the income and a beneficiary of the principal when the income-beneficiary dies
avoids probate	does not avoid probate

Now take a quick look at their differences and how the irrevocable _inter-vivos_ trust and the testamentary trust compare.

Note that irrevocable _inter-vivos_ trusts may reduce income tax as well as estate tax. Irrevocable trusts get their own tax identification number and file their own ax returns. Like corporations, they become new entities, separate from you—a legal clone. That entity (not you, the settlor) pays the income tax. One of the advantages is that if the trust is in a lower tax bracket than you are, it will owe less tax than you on the same amount of income.

But beware; there is a catch to that possibility. Tax bites are measured by *two* factors—the tax rate and the tax bracket. The tax rate applicable to the taxable income of a trust is the same as that applied to married persons filing separate returns. This rate is higher than those applicable to single individuals, heads of household, or married persons filing joint returns. Therefore, income tax will usually not be reduced by virtue of the trusts tax *rate*, since it will, most likely, have a higher rate than yours.

Income tax is usually reduced, however, because the trust has less reportable income than you. If your income-producing assets are less than the trusts (for example, your money is in real estate or nondividend paying stock) or your income is from tax-free bonds, it is possible for the trust to pay a higher income tax (in dollars) than you do.

16

USING REVOCABLE OR *INTER-VIVOS* TRUSTS TO AVOID PROBATE

Among the most popular methods of avoiding probate is the revocable trust, also called the living or "*inter-vivos*" trust. This type of trust was made famous by Dacey's *How to Avoid Probate* and the more recent *Loving Trust* by Esperti and Peterson. These trusts are touted by their admirers as the only right way to leave money to your heirs and indeed, there are good reasons for such devotion. Here are some advantages. You are able to:

- avoid probate.

- get professional management and test it during your lifetime.

- manage the money yourself and appoint a family member to take over upon your death without court interference.

- maintain privacy.

- have the trust continue after your death and keep the money managed for your heirs.

- provide for money management while you are alive if you become incompetent.

What the revocable trust does *not* do is save taxes or protect your assets from spend-down if you need long-term health care.

Now let's see what a revocable trust really is. It is a document under which you (the grantor) transfers assets to the trustee (also usually you) to manage on behalf of the income beneficiary (also you). Upon the grantor's (your) death, a successor trustee (usually your spouse or major beneficiary) takes over and distributes the funds as set forth by you in the trust document. In this way, there is no need to go to court to appoint an executor to distribute the funds of the deceased. With no need for an executor, there is no need for probate. This is how a revocable trust avoids probate, yet allows you to handle your money throughout your lifetime.

As an extra added attraction, you can include a power of attorney in the revocable trust that will allow your attorney-in-fact to take over without a court order if you become incompetent. (In Key 23, you will learn about the powers of attorney.) Any of these types described can be incorporated in the revocable trust.

Moreover, any tax-saving clause that can be placed in a will can also be placed in a revocable trust. Be aware that while many professionals are familiar with the use of these trusts to avoid probate, not all are sophisticated enough to combine the document with tax-saving clauses. Make sure the agenda includes tax savings.

And that's all there is to it! A graphic of a revocable trust would look like the flow chart at the end of this Key.

Yet, this traditional device can permit the trustee (usually you, during your lifetime) to:

- run a business.

- give to charity.

- invest.

- spend.
- hold any kind of property.

In short, you can do anything you would do with the money and property if there was no trust. If you wish, the trust can be freely amended and even revoked. It can contain a trust that continues after the death of the grantor (you). A successor trustee is named in the trust to perpetuate it through a second and sometimes third generation. All states have rules limiting the length of a trust so it does not last in perpetuity.

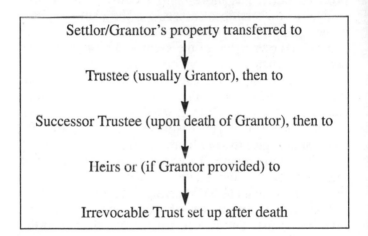

Settlor/Grantor's property transferred to

Trustee (usually Grantor), then to

Successor Trustee (upon death of Grantor), then to

Heirs or (if Grantor provided) to

Irrevocable Trust set up after death

17

USING IRREVOCABLE TRUSTS TO AVOID PROBATE

An irrevocable trust is another device that avoids probate, but it has more lasting consequences with respect to ownership of assets. As the name implies, money and property placed in such trusts are out of the control and ownership of the grantor. The grantor does not act as trustee. The grantor cannot revoke the trust at will, although some states permit revocation with the consent of all beneficiaries under limited circumstances.

For property that you wish to permanently transfer (but not outright) to your heirs, an irrevocable trust can serve to avoid probate. It also takes the appreciation of the assets out of your estate. We will discuss the irrevocable trust again as a tax-saving device in Key 32.

For probate avoidance, it works exactly like the revocable trust. The named trustee can distribute the assets in accordance with the wishes of the grantor at death or even prior thereto, depending on the directions. No will nor executor is necessary, and therefore no probate need take place.

However, for tax purposes the differences are vast. A revocable trust in which you are named as grantor and trustee needs no separate tax identification number. Your social security number will be sufficient, and all taxable gains are entered on your personal tax return.

An irrevocable trust needs its own tax identification number, obtained from the IRS after the trust document is drawn. The trustee files a yearly tax return on behalf of the trust, and the retained income is taxed to the trust, with any income distributed to beneficiaries taxed to them. Income that is ordinarily tax-free, such as municipal bond income, remains tax-free even if the trust owns the asset.

In summary, an irrevocable trust avoids probate in the same way that a revocable trust does. The assets transferred, however, are no longer in control of the grantor. Special clauses outlined in Key 34 can give the grantor the right to keep an income stream for limited periods of time. The trust gets the growth or appreciation of the asset out of the grantor's estate, saving estate taxes. The trust keeps the income not received by the grantor out of the grantor's income tax return, which saves taxes.

Many of the following Keys will discuss specific types of irrevocable trusts. They are used to save estate and income tax and protect assets in the event that long-term health care is needed and are given to charity. They require the services of professional money managers.

18

WHAT TYPE OF PROPERTY IS BEST PLACED IN A TRUST?

The type of assets you decide to place in a trust, whether revocable or irrevocable, depends on your goals. When you review the following list, if you are like most people, you will find that you share many of the goals. Once you get used to a trust, you may find that you place all your property in trusts for many different reasons. Goals might include:

- to avoid probate

- to reduce estate taxes

- to reduce income taxes

- to have money managed during your lifetime

- to have money managed after your death

- to be eligible for government benefits for long-term care.

Let's look at each goal and see how it relates to the type of asset best placed in a trust.

To avoid probate: When assets are in one person's name alone and that person dies, there must be a probate (if there is a will) or an administration (if there is not a will). In either case, the fiduciary (executor or administrator) must make an inventory of all the probate assets. In some states the fiduciary must even inventory joint and other assets that will avoid probate.

Shocking as it may seem, some states even base the fiduciary's fee on a percentage of all assets, probate and nonprobate. This means that if you created a trust and put some but not all of your assets into it, you still need a probate proceeding for those that remain in your name. Once this begins, a fiduciary may be entitled to include even the trust, joint, or other probate-avoiding assets in determining the fee. The assets will still avoid probate, but they will result in an inflated fee to the fiduciary. If the fiduciary is a loved one taking no fee, this will not mean much to you, but if you have appointed a bank or a professional, it can unnecessarily cost your estate a great deal of money.

In sum, to completely avoid probate you should have all of your assets in a revocable trust or in a designation-of-beneficiary format, as described in Keys 16 and 8. Funds in an irrevocable trust, created to save taxes, will also avoid probate. In order to raise your consciousness about types of assets, here is a partial list of an inventory required at probate: bank accounts, certificates of deposit, checking accounts, money market accounts and funds, municipal bonds treasuries, stocks, commodities, limited partnerships, corporate and business partnership shares, cars, boats, planes and all other vehicles, furniture, jewelry, real estate, coins, stamps, art, collectibles, paycheck. This is a short book, but you should get the idea.

To reduce estate taxes: If your goal is to save estate taxes, the assets you place in a revocable trust will save nothing. Only those items placed in an irrevocable trust will be considered out of your ownership and control at the time of your death, and therefore out of your estate. When you choose to transfer for this purpose choose assets that:
1. you don't mind relinquishing forever.
2. are appreciating so that the growth is out of your estate.

3. do not have a low basis (a low original acquisition price plus costs of improvements).

Now that you know the rules, let's see why they are that way. First, you don't want to give up property from which you need the income or that you plan to use. In limited cases (discussed in Keys 34 and 38) you will learn how to transfer certain assets irrevocably but still get limited use of investment income.

Second, because the value at the time you transfer an asset to an irrevocable trust is counted against your unified credit (see Key 27), the real savings in transferring to an irrevocable trust comes from keeping the future appreciation out of your estate. That makes stocks, real estate, and other "winner" assets perfect candidates for such transfers.

Third, property you consider transferring should not have a low basis. Basis is defined as the sum of the price you originally paid for an asset, the cost of acquiring the asset (legal and brokers fees), and improvements made. Until the law changes, your heirs get a bonus if you keep low basis property and leave it to them upon your death. The bonus is called a stepped-up basis. After they inherit, the basis of the property is stepped up from your low basis to the higher date-of-death value. If your heirs sell, they pay capital gains tax only on the difference between the sale price and the date-of-death value. Don't save estate taxes for the family by transferring low basis property, which will result in higher income taxes when your heirs sell. Your accounting professional must be asked to do the comparison for you.

To save income taxes: An irrevocable trust is the only trust to use when your purpose is to save income taxes. Once again you must be careful to transfer only assets that you no longer wish to control. For example, suppose you have income from a second mortgage on a house that you sold and it pays a high interest rate. If you are not using this income, it is appropriate to transfer the mortgage to the ownership of an irrevocable trust, naming your children as income beneficiaries. As the borrowers pay back, the income is distributed directly to the children, who can use the money and pay tax at their rate. If you die before the mortgage is paid off, the remaining debt is not counted in your estate. You can, of course, just give the mortgage to the children, but a trust also permits you to put certain restraints on the distribution.

To have money managed for you: This goal needs little explanation. If you believe your heirs or loved ones cannot handle assets, or if you would like to put someone else in charge of your assets even while you live, a trust is the right vehicle.

To be eligible for government help in the event you need long-term care: The subject of Medicaid benefits and asset protection is beyond the scope of this book. Some trusts can help you although the laws limiting them change frequently. The amount you would have to transfer to be eligible for government help varies from state to state. To learn more see *How to Budget Your Life Savings* by Harley Gordon (Financial Planning Institution, Inc., 1991).

For various reasons, you may be transferring a good many of your assets to a trust: How is it done? That will be discussed in the next Key.

19

TRANSFERRING ASSETS TO A TRUST

No matter how legally correct, a trust will have no effect if no assets are transferred to it. Odd as it may seem, a startling number of people create trusts and fail to make transfers. Often, clients are given a choice. Paralegals may handle the transfers or the client can be instructed in how to do it. Some transfers, however, like transfers of real estate, must be handled by an attorney. The following instructions may help you determine the most economical way to proceed. Remember: transferring assets to a trust simply means placing the asset in the name of the trust. All procedures are designed to achieve that end both legally and quickly.

Bank Accounts — Take a signed copy of the trust to your bank and have the bank change the name on the account to read "(name), as trustee of the trust of (date)." If the bank uses different language, go along with that procedure, and if it seems odd, check with your attorney. Don't be surprised if the bank keeps a copy of the trust in a confidential file. Perhaps it will accept just the first and last pages for even greater confidentiality. If the trust is revocable, use your own social security number. If the trust is irrevocable, your attorney will have applied for a trust tax identification number from the IRS. If you don't have it, tell the banker that an application is pending and supply it later.

Once you have done this you can continue to do all that you wish with the money including spending it, writing checks, and making withdrawals. If the trust is irrevocable, the trustee must sign all documents and can control the funds in accordance with the powers assigned in the trust document.

Stocks and Bonds — To transfer registered securities, each owner must sign the back of all stock certificates in their possession. If the broker holds the shares, obtain a stock power to sign. Submit them to the transfer agent whose name is on the back of the certificate or have your broker do it. All signatures must be guaranteed by a bank or brokerage house. This is done by having an official at your bank guarantee your signature from one already on file. Send all documents registered or certified mail.

For securities held by your broker, whether registered in your name on the books of the corporation or in street name (the name of your brokerage firm on the books of the corporation), simply ask your broker to open a new account in the name of the trust and transfer the assets to the account. If you take delivery later, you may simply have them reregistered in the name of the trust. The simplicity is worth any service charge you might pay. But a warning: Be sure the transfer is not a sale of the securities. Ask your broker to confirm that it is not.

As with the bank accounts, you can do anything you choose as trustee of your revocable trust. If there are different trustees, they must abide by the trust powers clause. If you want them to be able to buy on margin or trade options, spell it out in the trust.

Real Estate — It is strongly recommended that a law firm handle these transfers. A new deed is executed by you (as owner) to you (as trustee of the revocable trust), or to another trustee of the irrevocable trust. The deed must then be recorded in the county where the property is located. In many states, the trust document must be recorded, too. For privacy and to save recording fees (often charged by the page), a one-page synopsis of the trust is usually filed.

Be sure to discuss any real estate transfer taxes that may be incurred by transferring property to a trust. Generally, they are not imposed when the transfer is to a revocable trust, but check with your lawyer. Read your mortgage to see if you must inform the bank of the transfer (usually yes) and if the bank can elect to call the mortgage (with a revocable trust, usually no).

If (for tax or other reasons) it is inconvenient to record the new deed, you can leave an unrecorded deed in the file in most states. Your successor trustee will file it at your death and the property will be handled in accordance with the trust provisions.

Business Interests — Transferring business interests depends entirely on the nature of your interest. Partnership agreements and all partnership documents must be changed. Stockholders' agreements and the registration of closely held shares must be changed. Sole proprietorships require a review of all records (including checking accounts) for changes. Once again, you are advised to hire an accountant or attorney to counsel you.

Government Securities — To transfer your interest in treasury bond, notes, EE, HH, and other government securities, write to the Bureau of Public Debt, 999 East Street NW, Washington, DC 20007. They will mail you the latest rules.

Other Property — Cars, boats, and other vehicles require a change in the certificate of ownership and a visit to the motor vehicle bureau for reregistration.

Tangible property such as pianos, jewelry, art, antiques, and collectibles often do not have any documents showing ownership. Instead, the trust contains a general clause transferring all noncash tangible personal property. If you wish to specify certain items, use an

Exhibit or attach a list to the trust and refer to it in the trust. In that way, you can change the list without changing the whole trust.

Insurance Policies, Pensions and Assets that allow for a designation of beneficiary — In Keys 8 and 9, there are discussions of such assets. To have the trust terms apply, simply name the trust as the beneficiary.

If you forget to title property in the name of the trust, all is not lost. A type of will called a pour-over will can provide that any assets in your name alone will pour over into the trust and be distributed in accordance with its terms. These assets will, however, be probated. If they are small, you can use the simplified probate outlined in Key 6.

Your next step is to choose beneficiaries, and not everyone has an easy time choosing them. In the next Key, we will look at some strategies that can help.

20

CLAUSES RELATING TO BENEFICIARIES

Technically, a discussion on how to avoid probate or save taxes should not involve a discussion of beneficiaries. Practically, however, if you are concerned with whom to name as the object of your bounty, you will never get to the fine points of estate planning. Unfortunately, lawyers can tire of endless ruminations of family problems (or at least charge you by the hour as you complain about your spendthrift son or disappointing daughter, or worry over your handicapped child).

A wide variety of family situations follows, from second marriages to charities, along with some legal strategies to solve problems that hamper sophisticated planning.

Beneficiaries That Never Do What You Want or Are Always in Trouble — In a trust or in a will, you can leave a gift on certain conditions (a beneficiary must stop drinking, get married, stop taking drugs, or even practice a specific religion). The possibilities are endless, but certain requirements apply:

- The condition must not be against public policy (committing a crime or getting a divorce).

- The condition must be absolute and not a mere wish (be good to your sister and share with her).

- The condition must be specific, not vague (be of good moral character).

- The condition must have a discernable time limitation (never divorce—this is too vague; What do we do if the beneficiary never gets a divorce, but dies still married?)

- The condition can be required to take place before the inheritance is given on penalty of forfeiture of inheritance if the condition is violated (drinking again).

Caveat: State law dictates public policy. Ask your lawyer if the condition you want is permissible. Don't forget to provide for a back-up beneficiary if the condition is not met.

Beneficiaries Who Cannot Handle Money — Whether the beneficiary is incompetent, handicapped, frail, or a spendthrift, the trust is a helpful tool. Trusts can be set up in a will to take effect on your death or be an *inter-vivos* trust that is set up during your lifetime. The funds can be managed for the beneficiary while you are alive so you can test how it's working. If you are already satisfied with the strategy, you can create a probate avoiding trust as set forth in Key 15, which provides that your successor trustee place assets in another trust when you die, to be managed for your beneficiary.

If your problem is that you don't have an available trustee, see the ideas in Key 21.

Spouses Who Need Special Protection — Often your primary beneficiary is your spouse and you would like to leave everything to him or her. In Keys 35 and 36, you will discover some tax reasons not to do so. But some of you may also have other reasons, for example your spouse cannot handle money, your spouse is prey to the demands of a child with few scruples, or your spouse is receiving government entitlements. In all of these cases, a trust that limits the receipt of funds to income only, but still qualifies for the marital tax saving deduction, can be of use. See Key 36 for the so-called QTIP (qualified terminable interest trust) that can be placed in a will or in an *inter-vivos* probate-avoiding trust.

Divorces, Second Families, Stepparents — The flexible family is here to stay. If your child is in the custody of an ex-spouse, it doesn't mean that your money has to be. Put the funds marked for your children into a trust that takes effect upon your death, naming whomever you choose as trustee. Even if your ex-spouse predeceases you, the money will never be handled by the stepparent. This is true even if you gave up parental rights and allowed an adoption.

If you are the one that has remarried, whether or not you have custody of the children and whether they are minors or adults, a good idea is a nuptial agreement that makes clear whether or not the new spouse has relinquished all rights to your estate. These rights or elective shares equal one-third of your assets in most states.

Before a waiver of rights is signed, you and the new spouse can design any arrangement that seems fair, including giving the house to the kids and a lifetime lease to the new spouse.

Your Children Are Very Unequal in Their Abilities to Earn or Handle Money, or Are Very Erratic in the Way They Live — Again a trust, this one called a sprinkling trust, permits the trustee to sprinkle funds around differently according to the varying needs of the children and to change arrangements as their circumstances change. It is even possible to have one child act as trustee for the other. Some obvious drawbacks are discussed in Key 21.

You Are Single and Have No Beneficiaries — A striking lack of knowledge in the area of charitable giving plagues this country. It keeps money from legitimate charities, deprives donors of excellent tax-planning strategies, and (at worst) allows money to go to the unscrupulous. See Keys 37–38 for an eye-opening review of such circumstances.

Your Beneficiary Is an Unmarried Mate of the Same or Opposite Sex — No state as yet recognizes the rights of unmarried mates. But total protection is available through the use of wills, trusts, and designation of beneficiaries. Such voluntary bequests are unassailable except by a validly married surviving spouse who asserts his or her marital statutory share (one-third in most states).

In your efforts to save taxes and avoid probate, don't forget that the *most* important aspect of estate planning is distribution of assets to the right people in the right way. Make sure you and your advisors give as much thought to your beneficiaries as you do to Uncle Sam. An often difficult issue is who will manage assets on behalf of your beneficiaries. See the next Key for some ideas.

21

HOW TO CHOOSE TRUSTEES

Whom to appoint as trustee? The answer is different for everyone. Remember that the job of the executor ends when the will has been probated. On the other hand, the job of the trustee continues until the trust is terminated, which may be several years and perhaps a lifetime. Because of this, big institutions, banks and fiduciary organizations are all waiting in line to be appointed as trustees. Don't forget family lawyers, who also make part of their living from serving as trustee.

Many people consider a brother-in-law or a friend who is smart in business as possible trustees of both *inter-vivos* and testamentary trusts. Often the problem of choosing trustees brings about family tensions. It is also commonplace for male chauvinism to crop up. Frequently, a husband has made a will leaving substantial amounts to his wife, but thinks that she is incapable of handling the estate. The result is that sometimes an incompetent male relative is appointed instead of the wife, who is given no right in the will to get rid of him and she suffers as a consequence.

On the other hand, not every spouse, male or female, would make a good trustee. You may have to seriously consider your view of your spouse and only you know what gives you peace of mind. It generally does not work to appoint other relatives as trustees, because no one likes to be at the mercy of a family member. People are reluctant to give information to their in-laws, or worse, to their in-laws' spouses. You are probably going to want a paid professional, at least one—maybe even two. A suggestion is co-fiduciaries—one of them the major beneficiary (such as your spouse) and the other a paid professional.

Then there is the second question: Whom should I use as a paid professional, an institution or an individual? Believe it or not, it may be wise to use both. The institution has the double advantage of continuity and personnel. It may have a large team of experts, so should one expert leave or die, someone will be there to take over immediately.

The individual has the advantage of offering service, understanding, and intimacy. An individual lawyer who knows the family and is sensitive as well as knowledgeable can singlehandedly make the investment suggestions best suited to individual cases. Remember that large institutions do not plan for you alone. They often have hundreds of other clients and make mass investment strategies.

The individual knows you personally and treats you separately. Individual experts may also be more in need of your business. They need you because you may make up one percent, instead of one-millionth of one percent, of their business.

Of course there's a drawback. Individual trustees may discover problems they can't handle and have to hire other experts to help, using your money. Also, they may have no one to take over if they should become disabled.

Today, the practicalities of estate practice are such that no one can really handle it alone. Even those who appear to be individual estate planners work with accountants, pension planners, ERISA specialists, and sometimes even other lawyers to make a complete plan. When you talk to your lawyer, ask about the back-up staff. You may be surprised.

One solution is the double and even triple fiduciary

relationship. The major beneficiary is appointed a trustee together with an institution and an individual counselor. The individual counselor keeps up the dialogue with the institution and has equal authority. The institution uses its expertise for investment.

Your individual lawyer can work immediately and will listen to your wishes and react quickly; there is no bureaucracy. That doesn't mean you'll get your way, it just means you'll be able to voice your opinion and as a fiduciary, have a vote.

Conflicts can always occur, even between institutions and individuals—sometimes *especially* between institutions and individuals. The solution to this is simple. The institutions consist of highly professional people and the individual you choose must be a highly professional person. Get them together early. Have them meet with and without you. Clients sometimes send their attorney to lunch with a bank manager or trust officer of the institution they have chosen. They then develop a relationship and if something happens to the institutional fiduciary, the lawyer has been there all along and can educate whoever takes over. The reverse is also true.

Using the co-trustee may be just the way to keep a widow in touch with the money that is rightfully hers and still have her working side by side with a professional. She should also have the right to fire the professional if the work is not being done properly, as long as she appoints another immediately. The problem with co-trustees is that they are both equal fiduciaries. The widow may feel small and unimportant next to the big, powerful corporation that is her co-trustee and she may be discouraged from participating. In turn the corporate trustee begins to take over and make investment decisions without consultation. The answer is to prepare your beneficiary. One good way is reading this book. To help co-fiduciaries further along, have an emergency clause for illness or disability, a delegation clause for temporary absence, and a hold-harmless clause if one trustee (like the shy spouse) doesn't participate. There can even be a difference-of-opinion-clause in case there is an impasse. Majority rule is possible. Or something like this:

> In the event of a difference of opinion the (corporate) (individual) trustee's decision shall apply, provided it is given in writing to the other. The (corporate) (individual) trustee shall abide by the decision of the other and shall not be liable for the actions of the trustees made pursuant to the decision.

Use the individual as a special trustee with review powers for sprinkling, accumulation, or invasion. For example, an attorney can be named as trustee for the sole purpose of determining whether income should be accumulated or distributed between beneficiaries, or even whether the principal should be invaded. An institution can have investment control. Be flexible and creative. Most things can be done. Just remember, in judging fiduciaries the criteria are:

1. *Continuity* — Will they be around long enough so that no one else has to stop and choose the fiduciary after you're gone?
2. *Consistency* — Is it an institution that changes personnel all the time or is it an individual who passes you off to subordinates?
3. *Conversation* — Is there a dialogue among you, your beneficiary, and your fiduciary—a willingness to talk?
4. *Calculation* — How have they done in the past with other people's money? They will be able to give you some idea without breaching the confidentiality of their other clients.

If you want to use a professional or institutional trustee, you'll learn what to look for in the next Key.

22

HOW TO CHOOSE BANKS OR OTHER INSTITUTIONS AS TRUSTEES

Once you decide on using a bank or other institution as your fiduciary, you have to take the next step and decide which bank to choose. Most of us are ill-equipped to judge institutions, but good judgment and common sense are all you need.

How to judge a bank? Start with the people. How will the bank assign personnel to you to handle your account? The best institutions try to match customers to account executives and trust officers. Ideally, customers with similar needs will be served by the same person, someone who has expertise in the needed area. Ask the procedure for switching within the bank if you're not satisfied. Don't be shy about this; it can and does happen.

Talk to the people at the bank (or other institution) and have your spouse speak with them too. Watch the kind of advertising and outreach they are doing with the public. As with lawyers, there is no reason for an institution to create an image that it doesn't really want. Banks are not shy in disclosing the kind of business they want. It's up to you to express the kind of service you want.

Also compare the investment policies at various banks and institutions. For example, do they use their own common funds as the vehicle for investing money in a trust for which they have been named as trustee? They will give you performance records if you ask for them.

Request three to five years' worth. Compare them with the performance records of other common funds. Use the following indicators, which can be found in your newspaper, for comparison: Dow Jones Industrial Average, Standard & Poor's Composite Index, New York Stock Exchange Index. Also ask what type of fund is being used. Is it one that emphasizes income, growth, or tax free returns?

Also compare requirements for accepting you. Most institutions will not take a trust and act as trustee unless there is a specified amount of money in the trust. Some banks, however, actively seek individual trust accounts and are flexible. Some may take a smaller trust if it is not a complex one and if it fits in easily with the kind of management they are accustomed to.

See how institutions act with your individual co-trustees. For the most part, they will insist on being paid as much as they would be if they were sole trustees. There are few variations, but you might look around.

Even more important is the relationship between the family member or individual lawyer named as trustee, and the bank. Observe the dialogue that they set up with each other. This is particularly important if you have special assets to manage like copyrights and royalties.

If you are considering a bank and simply want to test the water, there are two ways to proceed before you name a permanent trustee. The first step in the process is to open an advisory account. The account should be totally in your control and no trust should be set up. But the bank does give investment advice and handles your investments. The charge is slightly higher than for acting as trustee because it is not limited by statute. In states without statutory limitations the charges may be the same. It is the investment advice in which you are interested, so familiarizing yourself with a bank's investment performance can be of considerable importance.

A second method of testing the water is to set up a revocable trust. This is one way to judge the performance of any trustee.

Finally, no reputable trustee will prevent you from including a discharge clause in your trust document. While you might find it necessary or desirable to change the trustee, it is also possible the trustee will wish to renounce that role during the course of the trust. Usually, however, when that is the case, the trustee will simply not qualify at the time the *inter-vivos* trust is created or the will is probated. Either eventuality gives another good reason to think carefully about your substitute trustees.

A few words now about costs. The expense of multiple trustees is not necessarily forbidding. Some states don't permit lawyers to double charge, that is, they can't charge legal fees and fiduciary fees. Usually the legal fees are greater and prevail.

Some states provide statutory limits for charges by fiduciaries based upon the amount of principal in a trust each year. New York provides that three trustees must share the fee of two trustees if the trust is valued at between $100,000 and $200,000. If the trust is valued at more than $200,000, each trust is entitled to one full statutory commission unless there are more than three, in which case a total of three commissions is apportioned.

So you might pay the same amount as you would if you had only one institutional fiduciary and still needed legal work. Banks and other institutions will provide rate schedules on demand, but they will also require yearly minimum fees or they won't take your account.

Before you make a final decision, do the following when deciding among large institutions:

- Look for lawyers on the staff.
- Question the fiduciaries about the complexity of assets they are used to handling.
- Pick an institution that has experience in operating in all of the localities where you have assets and beneficiaries.
- Ask your lawyer to advise you and encourage coordination.
- Introduce your beneficiaries to the fiduciary and consider their response.

You can only do your best. Once you make the decision, don't second guess and aggravate yourself. There is no absolutely perfect choice.

23

POWERS OF ATTORNEY

Powers of attorney have nothing to do with attorneys, but they have a good deal to do with power. A power of attorney is a document that names another person as your substitute in the event that you are unable to act for yourself with regard to a financial, legal, or real estate matter. You can be creative and name an attorney-in-fact—which is what the person or institution that you name is called—to do almost anything legal on your behalf, from signing a check to running your business.

Today, powers of attorney are a popular estate planning tool, while in the past they were used by the wealthy and healthy to give over power while they rested in Europe or took the grand tour. For this reason, traditional powers of attorney were unsuitable when the average person required them for estate purposes. Several useful variations on the traditional power have been created to meet modern needs. Some are discussed here. While they are simple documents, they are very important and you should be familiar with all your choices:

1 *The general power of attorney* gives the power to do anything, including signing your name to checks and contracts, that you would be able to do. The document is far-reaching and dangerous unless your attorney-in-fact is acting totally in your benefit.

2. *The specific power of attorney* gives only a limited power as described in the document. For example, if you have created a revocable trust,

one of your options might be to sign a limited power of attorney allowing the attorney-in-fact to transfer assets only to the trust. After that, the terms of the trust would apply in guiding the use of the assets.

3. *The durable power of attorney* is really a special clause in a specific or general power. It states that if you become incompetent the power will still be in effect.

Caveat: Without this durability clause, the power becomes ineffective as soon as you become legally incompetent to handle your own matters. Ironically, many people sign a power just to avoid a court conservatorship proceeding, in the event that they get Alzheimer's disease or are otherwise incapacitated. Yet, unless the power has the durability clause, the power will not serve this purpose.

---

4. *The springing power of attorney* is a general or specific power that only becomes effective when you become incompetent. It remains dormant while you handle your affairs, then springs to life upon incompetency.

From this discussion two questions arise: (1) What is incompetency? and (2) Who shall I use as my attorney-in-fact? You have the legal power to determine both answers.

Medical and legal incompetency have different meanings. Further, the meaning varies from state to state and in the context of the question. For example, legal incompetency to commit a crime may be different from legal incompetency to handle your money. You, in the power of attorney, can give the definition of what incompetency means to you. Only if this definition is fulfilled will the springing power or other incompetency-related provision be effective. Many clients simply rely on the written statement of two doctors given to the attorney-in-fact. If the attorney-in-fact is acting too soon, a proceeding can be brought to stop the use of your funds by you or anyone else with a clear interest in your welfare. It could be, for example, a beneficiary, a spouse, or other, perhaps an interested friend or relative. The attorney-in-fact will be stopped if the definition you dictated is not met.

Even so, you don't want to have to watchdog the person or institution you appoint. Reread the sections on trustees in Keys 21 and 22 because the discussions on selecting trustees, either an individual or a bank or other financial institution, applies here as well.

In addition, don't forget that you should also name successor attorneys and co-attorneys in cases where they are warranted.

24

HOW TO HANDLE ASSETS IN OTHER STATES AND COUNTRIES

Perhaps the most compelling reason to avoid probate using a revocable trust is the so-called "ancillary probate" of out-of-state or out-of-country property. The courts in the state where the decedent was domiciled at the time of death do not have jurisdiction to probate such property. The executor must bring an ancillary proceeding where the property is located. In many states and foreign countries the following costly procedure applies:

1. Someone must be designated to represent the estate that has an office in the jurisdiction. This usually means hiring a second attorney admitted to practice where the property is located, that attorney acting as the resident agent.

2. A second or ancillary probate must be conducted including extra fees and sometimes holding up the main proceeding in the home state. The ancillary probate cannot begin until the probate at the domicile has commenced and the executor appointed by that court. Many ancillary probates prolong the total procedure for a year because they cannot be conducted simultaneously with the main probate.

3. Some jurisdictions require the main fiduciary to appoint another (in-state) fiduciary. Once again, a lawyer or institution must be paid a fee for this service.

These rules apply even if the property in another state is of minor value. They always apply to real estate located in the jurisdiction. If you own a second home, you must be particularly careful to use a joint deed with right of survivorship in order to avoid probate. Better yet, place the property in a revocable probate-avoiding trust.

If the property is in another country, even more complications occur. Some attorneys have traveled internationally on many occasions to straighten out foreign estate problems. You certainly don't want to finance such travel if it can be avoided.

Should you use a trust to avoid ancillary proceedings, it must conform to the laws of the state where the property is located, not to the state of domicile. The best thing to do is make a separate trust when you purchase out-of-state or foreign property. Some countries will not recognize United States laws, but most will give comity (the international equivalent of full faith and credit) to our laws.

Once again, these considerations help avoid double probate but have no effect on your taxes. In some cases, both the state of domicile and state of location of property will tax the asset. In other instances, one jurisdiction gives credit for taxes paid to another. Only your accountant at the time of planning can advise you.

Speaking of taxes, we will be looking at estate and gift taxes, after the probate summary in the next Key.

25

WHAT ARE ESTATE TAXES?

The Internal Revenue Code, the federal statute that provides the basic laws of taxation, contains a gift and estate tax section. The Internal Revenue Service, through rulings, regulations, memos, and private letter rulings, interprets that section. Tax courts illuminate, reverse, or uphold that interpretation when challenged by a taxpayer. Although it can get complex, gift and estate tax is one of the easier areas for the layperson to understand.

The estate and gift tax tables are the same. Taxes are imposed on all the assets that an individual owns or controls at the time of death, over and above an exemption of $600,000. Keys 26 and 28 will explain the concept of control and discuss the assets that are included in the estate. Persons with estates and gifts under $600,000 are not subject to the federal tax.

Unlike estate taxes, gift taxes can be paid during your lifetime, when you actually make the gift. You have a choice of (1) paying at that time, (2) waiting until your death and combining the gift and estate taxes, or (3) taking a credit against your $600,000 and paying no tax. Remember that the $600,000 is a lifetime exemption applying to both gifts and estate assets.

For gifts only, there is one additional exclusion. You can give up to $10,000 per year per beneficiary every year of your life and not use any of the $600,000 exemption or pay any tax. A husband and wife together can give up to $20,000 (as a couple) to as many beneficiaries per year as they like. The gifts will be tax free.

The rules that permit taking advantage of these exemptions while keeping the most control over the funds that the law allows, are the true essence of estate tax planning.

After reading the above, you may conclude that there is nothing to worry about when it comes to estate taxes. That may be true, but three things tend to make people with even small estates worry.

1. Once you do end up with any nonexempt dollars, the estate tax rate is very high. It begins at thirty-seven percent for the first taxable dollar and ends at fifty-five percent for estates over $3 million. The next Key, discusses calculating your tax.

2. Even if you are exempt from federal estate tax, you may not be exempt from state estate tax. You must check with your accountant, attorney, or other tax professional. The differences are vast from state to state. Usually you get the best break in the retirement (Sunbelt) states where this area of the law is designed to attract the older citizen.

3. Inflation and growth of assets is the third concern. With the new longevity apparent in our society, even a moderate estate has time to grow to impressive proportions. A $300,000 estate socked away at current interest rates could double in eight to ten years. In the past, a 65-year-old would be severely pushing the longevity table by age 73 to 75, but not today. It is likely that he (and especially) she could live another eight to ten years with a final estate of $1.2 million. The tax on that is almost $250,000.

Finally, you may find that estate tax planning is fun. Once you get familiar with it, you want to play all the right games by all the right rules. After all, it's your family fortune that you're saving. In the next Key, a method of making a rough calculation of your federal estate tax liability is described.

26

HOW TO CALCULATE ESTATE AND GIFT TAXES

The following is a very rough method of estimating your estate tax without using a computer or a tax professional. It comes with a warning: "Do not try this at home. The people you see doing it are trained professionals" (just like the television commercials for car performance). But you may find it useful to read this Key to get an idea of how the tax really works before you seek professional advice.

> *gross estate – administrative expenses = adjusted gross estate – marital deduction – charitable deduction = taxable estate + adjusted taxable gifts = tentative tax – gift taxes payable on such gifts – estate tax credits = net estate tax payable.*

What a formula! Now let's take a look at what each item is. As we do, you'll get a real feeling of how lifetime gifts and inheritance work together from the tax perspective.

Gross Estate — All property in the ownership and in the control of the decedent at the time of death is counted in the gross estate. In Key 29, you'll get an eye-opening look at how very comprehensive that inclusion is. In Key 29, you'll learn the meaning of ownership or control. For your present quick calculation, just add up all the assets you have today (often called your net worth). If you want to project into the future, pretend that you will live to age 84 (an actuarilly sound assumption) and use your own math skills or

tor to double your net worth every twelve

finer calculation, add four percent inflation each year. For an even finer calculation, take out the value of your primary residence from the net worth and guess at its approximate value at the date of death. This is suggested because the home does not follow the rules of doubling. Its eventual value depends on the real estate market in your area.

Expenses — From the gross estate, deduct administrative expenses. The deduction will differ widely between those who avoided probate and those who did not. Other deductible expenses include debts, funeral and burial costs, medical expenses, final care costs, executors fees and court, accountants and attorneys fees, along with all disbursements for telephone, fax, and other utilities.

The organization LIMRA (Life Insurance Marketing Research Association) estimates the average administrative costs nationwide, minus debts of the decedent, at $19,000.

Adjusted Gross Estate (AGE) — When the administrative expenses and debts are deducted from the gross estate, the result is the adjusted gross estate. The AGE is used to calculate marital and charitable deductions, certain tax-payment deferrals, and stock-redemption tax treatments (buying back stock from a family corporation).

Marital and Charitable Deductions — Each of these deductions are discussed in separate Keys, 35 and 41, respectively. One hundred percent of qualified marital and charitable gifts are deducted from the AGE to equal the taxable estate.

Adjusted Taxable Gifts — To the taxable estate, add all gifts given during your lifetime that exceed $3,000 per year per beneficiary before 1981, and $10,000 per year per beneficiary after 1981. Next, look at the estate and gift tax tables and get the tentative tax. Notice how those gifts you gave in the past are added to the decedent's estate before the tables are used. That is why the notion is repeated in several Keys that giving a gift only removes the gift's growth from the estate taxation, not the value of the gift itself. Note also that the yearly exclusions can save taxes if you limit your gifts to the excluded amounts.

Gift Taxes — What if you already paid a gift tax in the year you transferred nonexempt gift assets? You simply deduct the taxes you paid on the gifts from the tentative tax.

Estate Tax Credits — You may also deduct from the last figure several credits. They include foreign estate taxes paid, taxes paid on property inherited by the decedent within two years of death (check with your tax professional on this one), and a credit of $192,800 that is available to everyone.

The final result is the actual tax, if any, that you must pay. Let's go now to the next Key, where we will discuss the $191,800 tax credit.

27

WHAT ASSETS ARE INCLUDED AND WHAT ASSETS ARE EXCLUDED FROM TAX?

In general, all assets in the ownership and control of a decedent at the time of death are included in the gross estate, which forms the basis of the eventual tax. The concept of ownership and control is discussed further in Key 29.

Here we concentrate first on the concept of assets. Includable assets that you may not have considered are:

Jointly Held Assets — If you own assets in joint name with another person, the entire value will be counted in your estate unless the other person is your spouse. For most people, this fact is quite a surprise— they believe that only one-half the value will be counted.

To fight against the 100 percent inclusion, the survivors must show that they directly contributed to the assets. If the joint owners are husband and wife, the entire asset is excluded under the marital deduction, which is discussed later on.

Life Insurance — This is another surprising area. The value of the death benefit is included in the gross estate if the decedent had control over naming the beneficiary, borrowing against the policy, determining how dividends are applied, cancelling the policy, or receiving cash value. These are called incidents of ownership. To keep a policy out of the gross estate, you must name a different owner during your lifetime or transfer the policy to an irrevocable life insurance trust.

Assets Held in a Trust — As already stated in Key 16, a revocable trust saves you no tax because the assets are counted in your gross estate. But even an irrevocable trust that leaves you in control over the income or principal may be includable. Several subsequent Keys will give you advice on how to save taxes with trusts.

A Zoo of Mixed Assets — We tend to think of assets as things we can touch or easily quantify, like a home or a share of stock. But for estate tax purposes, items you may not consider assets are counted. Some are gifts of life insurance policies you made less than three years prior to your death (the entire death benefit is counted in the gross estate), powers of appointment (a power given to you in someone else's will or trust giving you the right to distribute their assets), a right of reverter greater than 5 percent of the property (the right to get property if someone who now has it breaches a condition of ownership), and income earned posthumously.

Now that you know the bad news about the inclusions, here is some of the good news:

Gift Tax Exclusions — You can give $10,000 each year to each beneficiary you choose. The number of yearly gifts are unlimited. Husbands and wives can give $10,000 per year to each beneficiary, even if only one holds the funds. For example, if the husband has a $20,000 bond in his name, he can give it, tax-exempt, to his son as long as the gift is from both Mom and Dad. These are called split gifts. Although a gift tax return must be filed in the year given, no gift tax must be paid.

Unified Credit — Each taxpayer has a lifetime

exemption of $600,000. This means that each person can give away (over and above the gift tax exclusion) or leave at death a sum not exceeding $600,000 without incurring an estate tax. As you can see from Key 26, this exemption is translated into a dollar-for-dollar credit from the tentative tax, before the final tax is determined. The $600,000 exemption from gross estate translates to a credit of $192,800. That is why you may read about a $600,000 exemption or a $192,800 credit. Don't be confused—they are the same thing.

In addition, assets are included in the gross estate. You should be aware that the valuation given to those assets has a great effect on the tax paid. The next Key concerns the most advantageous method of evaluating assets.

28

EVALUATING ASSETS FOR BEST TAX RESULTS

The size of an estate is determined by how its assets are evaluated. The executor is given a choice of evaluating assets (1) at death, (2) six months after death, or (3) on the date at which the asset is sold or distributed to a beneficiary (if either action took place within six months after death). To choose, the executor merely marks the proper box on the Federal Estate Tax return. The executor cannot change the selection once the time for filing, including extensions and paying of the tax, has elapsed. If the tax return is not filed on time the choice may be lost.

Any data, other than the date-of-death value, is called AVD, alternative valuation date. If the AVD is chosen for one asset it must be chosen for all.

Most of the time, the lowest value will result in the smallest tax. Sometimes for small estates, though, it is better to use the higher value. If an estate is small enough not to pay any estate taxes (less than $600,000 in net assets), a higher evaluation can save capital gains tax when the beneficiary sells the inherited asset.

For example, stock is worth $100,000 at the time of death and $120,000 six months later. By choosing the higher valuation, the heirs' taxable gain when the stock is sold will be based upon the difference between the sale price and $120,000, instead of $100,000. As long as the higher valuation does not render the estate taxable, income tax is saved and estate tax remains unchanged. Similar vigilance should be shown by executors who are handling the estate of someone who has died insolvent. It is important in such cases to watch the capital gains and less important to watch the estate taxes.

Distributions of property directly to heirs without a sale should be made *after* the six-month period has elapsed, unless the value of the property has declined a great deal before the six-month period. If the value has declined, distribute the property immediately at the time of its lowest value, within the six-month period after death. Some property, especially fluctuating stock, may increase in value if you wait. But the heirs get a stepped-up basis, which can increase their after-tax profit.

Reminder: Whenever you are making an evaluation decision, think about the other decisions you have to make and how they are affected. For example, if shares in a closed corporation are evaluated at their lowest value, they may not qualify for the special rules that permit taxes to be paid in installments (see Key 47). If installment payment is a goal, at least thirty-five percent of the gross estate must be comprised of stock of a closed corporation. The shares must not be valued so low that other assets in the estate bulk larger, and the corporate stock fails to meet the thirty-five percent requirement.

29

THE CONCEPT OF CONTROL IN ESTATE TAX PLANNING

From reading Key 26, you know that any asset in your ownership or control at your death is counted to determine your taxable estate. The operative word here is "or." An asset in your ownership will have your name on it, such as stocks, bonds, bank accounts, and deeds. But just because it does not have your name on it doesn't mean it is out of your estate.

For example, an insurance policy may be owned by your children. Yet if you kept the right to determine how the dividends are applied, to borrow against the policy, or to change the beneficiary, you are still in control. That policy's death benefit is counted in your gross estate. Some people transfer shares of stock to their heir's but they have a letter of agreement with their broker that they will control the investment. They also have an agreement with the heirs that the money will be used at their discretion and for their benefit. The IRS considers this a shame transfer and on audit will likely include the value of the asset in the gross estate. Other people do the same thing but put nothing in writing. The scheme often backfires when a creditor or estranged spouse of the heir makes a claim on the assets and, because they were fully transferred, gets a share. With nothing in writing, the transferee has no legal rights, but with something in writing the transferee still has control and the assets are subject to estate inclusion.

The moral of the story is to do things the fully acceptable legal way. As you will see, there are many legitimate ways to save estate taxes. In later Keys you will learn the best ways to use a trust to keep your rights in income from the assets, along with other useful devices.

For now it is important to mentally review the assets that you have given away (or thought you have) to see if you have unwittingly maintained control over them. Ask yourself these questions:

- "Did I keep any rights over my insurance policy?" If you are not sure, ask your agent.

- "Do I have money 'in-trust-for' or in joint accounts?" Neither are considered a relinquishment of control, and the entire asset is counted in the gross estate unless the beneficiary is a spouse.

- "Do I have a power of appointment—that is, the right to decide how another person's money or trust funds will be handled?" This is also a countable asset even if you don't appoint yourself as beneficiary.

- "Do my trusts allow me to control assets, get income all my life, demand principal, borrow against funds, and use my money for my own business or investment?" If so, even if they are irrevocable, the trust funds are counted in your gross estate.

More and more people want to transfer their assets, not to save estate taxes but to become eligible for Medicaid in case they need long-term or nursing-home care. While a complete treatment is beyond the scope of this volume, the next Key will present a background of the issue of control as it relates to Medicaid eligibility.

30

TRANSFERRING ASSETS TO BE MEDICAID-ELIGIBLE

With the blessed longevity we are experiencing comes the specter of frail old age that lasts through decades and wastes the family fortune. Medicare, to which all people over the age of 65 are entitled, and private health-care programs are two ways of paying for some of the costs. The other way is directly from the pocket book.

Because the costs of in-home care and nursing-home care are very high (in some regions $8000 a month), people are convinced that if they live too long, spending all their money is inevitable. The result has been a panicked transfer of assets while the transferer is still healthy. Many transfers are ill-designed and are really thinly veiled shams in which the transferers try to keep control of their money through under-the-table agreements with the transferees.

Remember that at this time, Medicaid is a social service (welfare program) and you must be needy to qualify. A problem arises when the children or other transferee take actual control over transferred assets and a healthy Mom and Pop find that they jumped from the frying pan into the fire. Moreover, many legitimate transfers are still not sufficient to establish eligibility. The very best thing to do is to have a consultation with an elderlaw specialist. Try the National Academy of Elderlaw Attorneys, located at 655 North Alverton Way, Suite 108, Tucson, AZ 85711 or your local bar association for referrals. Meanwhile, here is a quick sketch of the rules. This may demystify the area and alleviate any panic.

1. Rules are federal and state, so always check with an expert familiar with your own state program.
2. If you return to your home (or may be able to return to your home), you can keep your house, even if you have no spouse.
3. If you pay off your mortgage, the house stays yours free and clear and you have reduced your assets for Medicaid eligibility purposes.
4. Money you spend to fix up or expand your home also reduces countable assets, yet the home with its newly increased value is still yours.
5. Some states require that you obtain a doctor's report stating that you can return to the home some day or that you put a time limit on how long you can stay away; check on this.
6. If you have a spouse at home, almost all states give eligibility regardless of the value of the home as long as you otherwise qualify.
7. Wedding rings (regardless of their value and time they were bought), a car, $2,500 per spouse for burial, and $2,500 of the cash surrender value of life insurance policy are also excluded in most states.
8. A couple can have a minimum of $12,000 to a maximum of $62,000 in most states and still be eligible for Medicaid.
9. In most states, a court can increase the amount the spouse can keep and still have Medicaid eligibility for the spouse in need of care. For these hearings, you need an attorney specializing in the field.

Given these rules and the assets limitations, many people would like to transfer the excess assets that disqualify them to their children or other heirs. To do this, as with estate taxes, all ownership and control must be relinquished.

Even after a transfer of your assets, you are still not eligible for Medicaid unless one of two things has occurred: (1) thirty months or more has passed since the transfer or (2) the number of months derived by dividing the amount of assets you transferred by the monthly cost of the nursing home has elapsed. For example, if the home costs $6,000 per month and you transferred $60,000, then you will be Medicaid-eligible in ten months.

Finally, in many states, it is also possible to transfer property to a disabled dependent child, a spouse, or a sibling who is already a co-owner. This action will also help you qualify.

If you are still not eligible after all possible planning is done, you should look into long-term health-care insurance products. These products are improving and developing rapidly to meet the obvious need. Even if you have investigated it before, give your insurance agent another try.

Now that you have decided to transfer assets, either to save taxes or to qualify for Medicaid, you will want to consider the various ways to best make the transfer. The next Key looks at some unique methods of gift-giving.

31

THREE CATEGORIES OF TAX PLANNING

All of estate-tax planning falls into one of three categories. And if those three are not entirely successful, the fourth alternative is to pay the taxes. In the next several Keys we will look at the details of each strategy, but let's not miss the forest for the trees. The three categories are:

1. Give your assets away during your lifetime.
2. Give your assets to certain favored (by the Internal Revenue Code) beneficiaries upon your death.
3. Have your heirs do post mortem planning. If, after you have calculated the tax savings brought about by your plan and there is still a tax to pay, one good choice is to pay with insurance proceeds from a policy placed on an insurance trust that was purchased for that purpose.

Here is an overall view of each of the three tax-saving strategies.

Gift-Giving During Your Lifetime — As Keys 26 and 29 point out, assets not in your control when you die are not counted in your gross estate, and are therefore not taxed. One way to relinquish ownership and control of an asset is to give it away. For tax planning purposes the rules are simple:

• Each year you can give away up to $10,000 per recipient. That person need not have any special relationship to you.

- If you are a legally married couple, you can give up to $20,000 per person each year, even if you both do not contribute equally to the gift. You will have to file a gift-tax return, but you will pay no tax.

- In addition to the above tax-excluded gifts, you can also give away up to $600,000 during the course of your lifetime. As you use up this amount, you also reduce the amount you can leave tax-free at your death, because the $600,000 is for combined estate and given assets. In determining the dollar value of the gifts you give, the market value as of the date of transfer is used. Even if, by the time you die, the asset is worth more (or less), it's the value at the date of gifting that is used to compute how much of your $600,000 exemption you used.

- If, instead of giving the gift outright, you give it in a trust, it is not considered out of your estate as long as you keep control over the asset. This is the case with a revocable trust that gives you the power to amend the terms at will. If you are entitled to income from the trust, there are tax savings, but they are calculated in accordance with special rules discussed in Key 34.

- Finally, if you create a trust, each beneficiary is counted as one person. Therefore, you could give each person the usual $10,000 per year ($20,000 if you are a married couple) by transferring the assets to the trust. But you can't have it both ways. If the recipient is a trust beneficiary and you give a gift directly to the trust, that individual is not entitled to a second $10,000 tax exclusion with an additional personal gift in the same year.

Choosing Special Beneficiaries to Inherit Your Assets — Giving away money during your lifetime is not the only tax strategy available to you. Two types of beneficiaries have been selected by the drafters of the Internal Revenue Code (the Congress) for favored tax treatment. They are your spouse and your favorite charity.

You can leave any amount of assets upon your death to the person to whom you are legally married and none of it will be subject to federal estate tax. There is no limit. (Before 1981, there was a $250,000 or one-half of the estate, whichever was greater, limit.) If you have an old will or trust, reread it to be sure it does not have an old, pre-1981 clause. If it does, check with your attorney before it is redrafted.

Believe it or not, if you have other heirs (children that you want to protect, for example), it is not always the best idea to leave everything to your spouse, even the initial tax saving. A better strategy is found in Key 35.

The law also favors charitable beneficiaries. All assets given to a charity are exempt from estate tax, whether transferred at death or during your lifetime. The charity must be recognized as qualified by the terms of the Internal Revenue Code. Of course, you will want to check out the charity's worthiness. One way is to write to the National Charter Information Bureau, 19 Union Square West, New York, NY 10003-3395. Charitable gifts to trusts are also tax exempt. See Keys 37 and 38 for more details.

Postmortem Tax Planning — Sometimes there are still strategies that serve to save taxes after you are gone, yet you can plan for their use during your lifetime. They include renunciations, sometimes called disclaimers, in which your heir refuses or renounces an inheritance. This refusal can serve to save taxes under special circumstances. Your part is to put the right clauses in your will or trust to allow for this flexibility and to dictate who gets the asset if there is a renunciation. The benefits, method, and limitations are discussed in Key 43.

Sometimes You Just Must Pay — If you are fortunate to have such a large estate that you are unable to avoid all taxes, sometimes you just must pay. Even here, however, good planning can help. Some ideas include the following.

- Give gifts during your lifetime and pay the tax right away. This takes the tax money and its investment growth out of your estate.

- Buy an economical insurance policy like the second-to-die policies, discussed in Key 40, and have a trustee lend the proceeds to your executor to pay taxes. In this way you have liquidity and also keep the cash proceeds out of your gross estate (more about that in Key 39).

- Be sure that your assets are liquid so that real estate, art, and business assets need not be placed on distress sale to pay taxes.

- If 35 percent or more of your assets consist of a family business, you can take advantage of a tax payout, as discussed in Key 47.

You will find other tips and strategies throughout the next several Keys. Be sure not to mistake the tail for the dog—some people resent taxes so much that they overtransfer assets to heirs and impoverish themselves. And be careful to meet the other goals of estate planning—getting assets to the people you really love and staying financially independent throughout your own life.

32

REDUCING ESTATE
TAXES BY GIVING GIFTS
TO TRUSTS

The use of a trust to save estate taxes is entirely based on the principle of control, as explained in Key 29. Simply stated, the government only counts assets in your ownership and control at death as part of your gross estate. Assets not in your gross estate are not taxed. You can always give away assets outright, but in doing so, you relinquish all authority in the matter.

In order to make the best possible arrangements, the wealthy often give their assets to a trust, not an individual. The trust document, drafted by their lawyer under their instructions, gives directions for how the money is to be used, invested, and distributed; who runs the trust; and when the trust terminates. In this way, although the money is out of the gross estate, there are still restrictions that reflect the wishes of the grantor (the person who set up the trust).

Today, as we accumulate money because of longevity and inflation, the middle class is more interested in using a trust to save estate taxes. A trust is a document; it cannot be verbal. It transfers the grantor's property to the name of the trust, to be managed by a trustee appointed by the grantor and used for the benefit of those also designated by the grantor. These beneficiaries are the people, institutions, or charities that will have the benefit of the assets, according to the wishes of the grantor. They may be named (1) to receive income from the trust (income beneficiaries) or (2) to

get the remaining principal when the in
beneficiaries ceases due to death or othe
of that right (thus becoming remainderme)

Trusts used to avoid probate are expla
14, 15, 16, 20, and 21. Trusts to save taxes follow the
same rules; however, they must be irrevocable. Once
assets are transferred to the trust, the grantor must have
no personal right in the assets or the Internal Revenue
Service will argue that the assets should be included in
the gross estate.

To clarify how to approach the subject of trusts with
your attorney, here are the basic considerations. Some
of them may surprise you.

1. The trust must be made by you during your lifetime.
2. You must be competent when you make the trust
   and understand what you are doing.
3. While you are competent, you can give someone
   a power of attorney to transfer assets to the trust
   even after you become incompetent.
4. The trust must be irrevocable in order to save
   taxes.
5. If you decide you made a mistake, some states
   allow you and all your heirs to consent to a revocation.
6. The trustee is your choice but you cannot serve
   as a trustee unless you severely limit your own
   powers. You cannot use trust money for yourself,
   dependents, or business, nor may you borrow it,
   if you act as your own trustee.
7. The trustee cannot be under your control or the
   assets will be counted in your gross estate.
8. The trustee can be a beneficiary, bank, or professional individual (citizenship requirements vary
   from state to state).
9. Under the terms of the trust (a), it can terminate
   and all the money can be distributed to the

remaindermen when you die, or (b) the trustee can continue the trust until a certain date, event, or death of the beneficiary of income.

10. In no case can the trust last so long as to violate the rule against perpetuities. (The trust must terminate no later than 21 years after the last possible beneficiary of the trust, including those mentioned but yet unborn, dies. This is an interesting rule, but not worth going to law school to fully understand. Leave it to your attorneys and their word processors to draft the right clause, or see a video of the movie *Body Heat*, which features an incompetent lawyer who doesn't know The Rule Against Perpetuities.)

11. You choose the combination of beneficiaries that suit you, and you can make the contingencies; for example, they lose their beneficiary status if they move to another country or fail to marry.

12. Each year you can transfer up to $10,000 to each trust beneficiary, estate and gift tax-free. But this uses up the right to directly transfer tax-free to the same person that year.

These rules are relatively simple. There is, however, one special rule that's not so simple and is the essence of advantageous estate planning. This rule is called the present-interest rule. It holds that only property in which a beneficiary has a present interest qualifies as a completed gift to the trust. Therefore, if the beneficiaries must wait until they reach a certain age or achieve a certain goal before they benefit from the asset, it does not come under the gift exclusion.

Under a now-famous decision, *Crummey v. Commissioner* (397 F.2D 82, 9th Cir. 1968), a present interest is created if the beneficiary has the right to demand a distribution of assets, even if that person does not make the demand. If a beneficiary is a minor, an adult can be given power to make the demand on behalf of the minor and a present interest is

So far so good. All you have to do
Crummey power in a trust (the right to dem
and a present interest is created, even if t
not demanded. The status as a gift not counted in your
estate is preserved. Hooray.

But there is a catch. What if the beneficiary doesn't
take the money? This happens frequently when the
beneficiaries are minors. In that case, the Internal
Revenue Code (IRC) states that by declining the gift,
the beneficiaries have themselves given a gift. Each of
their $600,000 lifetime exclusions is debited by the
amount they could have demanded and didn't. Boo.

To the rescue comes another special rule called the
"5-by-5 rule." The IRC permits the beneficiaries to
decline $5,000 or five percent of the assets in the trust
each year, whichever is greater, and not have their
$600,000 exemption reduced. The IRC also does not
reduce your exclusion if you are the only beneficiary
of the trust. The rationale is that since your failure to
demand a distribution doesn't become anyone else's
benefit, there is no gift. You are just accumulating
more money for yourself for later.

Unfortunately, because of the complexity of the 5-
by-5 and *Crummey* rules, your trust will most likely
contain incomprehensible legalese. Your attorney,
however, is doing the right job. Fortunately, the rules
that apply to giving gifts to minors, as discussed in the
next Key, build upon the rules you have just learned.
So the worst is over.

33

REDUCING ESTATE TAXES BY GIVING GIFTS TO MINORS

Transferring assets to minors has long been the wealthy persons' way of keeping money in the family and reducing both income and estate taxes at the same time. Recently the Internal Revenue Code (IRC) put a crimp in their style by creating the so-called "kiddie tax" (to limit the reduction of estate tax). Nevertheless, the possibilities for tax reduction are good considering the limitations. There are four ways to transfer assets to minors but they all have one thing in common: Once the assets are transferred, the dividends or income derived from investing them will be taxed in a peculiar way if the minor is under the age of 14.

This is how the kiddie tax works. The first $600 a year of investment income is taxed at zero percent (no tax at all). The second $600 is taxed at fifteen percent—a big saving over the donor's tax bracket. The remaining yearly taxable income, if any, is taxed at the parents' marginal tax bracket (the highest rate the parents pay on their own income). This is true no matter who gives the gift—parent, grandparent, or whoever.

Therefore, when investing money for children, it is wise to choose assets that will generate no more than $1,200 a year in income and will be taxed very low. Place the remainder in tax-exempt or deferred assets if the parent is in a high tax bracket. When children reach the age of 14, they graduate to their own tax bracket. That is usually lower than the parents' and taxable investments become more appropriate.

To reduce estate taxes, you have already seen that a transfer of assets to get them out of your control works. Here are the four ways of making those transfers:

1. a direct gift to the child
2. a gift to a guardian to administer for the child
3. putting assets in joint names
4. creating a trust with the child as beneficiary

Direct gifts. The simplest means for transferring assets and income to a child is to make a direct gift. If stamps, jewelry, coins, and the like are given, there may have been a successful transfer but no guarantee that the asset will be invested or used as contemplated. If cash or other liquid assets are transferred, the minor can do little more than spend the money. In most states, a minor cannot create a trust, contract to hire a financial advisor, or even make a will. In some areas of the country, a minor cannot even rent a safe-deposit box. Therefore, before a direct gift is made, the minor's fiscal responsibility should be considered. Most parents and grandparents would not dream of making actual transfers to minors without exercising some control over the gift. Yet, even in states where 21 is the age of majority and where the teenager has shown fiscal responsibility, a direct gift may be appropriate and may help to psychologically cement a relationship. Above all, treat each situation individually; for example, it may be wise to invest money for one child who is an artist and transfer money to another who has an M.B.A.

Guardianships. Under a legal guardianship, a gift is given directly to the child with an adult controlling the money. Such arrangements can be accomplished through the Uniform Gift to Minors Act, joint ownership of assets, or custodial bank accounts.

The Uniform Gifts to Minors Act has been adopted by every state. It provides for the giving of money, securities, life insurance policies, or annuities to anyone under age 21. A custodian must be appointed to manage these gifts for the minor. Any adult family member, guardian, lawyer, or trust company may serve as a custodian. If a professional is appointed, a fee is paid; if a family member becomes the custodian, there is no fee. If the gift is money, life insurance policies, annuities, or registered securities, the donor may be appointed, but if unregistered securities are given, the donor may not act as the custodian.

The custodian is empowered to manage, hold, and invest the property of the minor and may sell or exchange this property if the proceeds are used for the minor's benefit. The custodian must also keep careful records, register all securities, and establish a bank account for the money. In short, this individual assumes all fiduciary responsibility for the property.

The minor assumes control of the money upon reaching the age of 21. If the minor dies before reaching that age, the money becomes part of the minor's gross estate. Once given, the gift is irrevocable; it belongs to the minor. Although the custodian (or donor) is empowered to control and manage the money, any tax due from earned income is assessed according to the rate of the trust, not at the rate of the custodian's personal income. If the donor dies before the minor reaches age 21, however, the property will accrue to the donor's estate and estate tax will have to be paid.

Joint Names. Clients often create joint ownership between themselves and a minor (child and grandchild). Many may do this without realizing they have created joint gifts. Here are a few examples:

• Open a joint bank account in both the parent's and child's name. A gift is considered to have been made (and tax incurred) when the other party withdraws money. No tax is incurred if each party contributes an equal amount.

- Purchase a United States Bond in two names. The purchaser may cash in the bond tax-free; the other party would pay a gift tax upon cashing it.

- Purchase joint stock. Naming a joint owner establishes that a gift has been made.

- Add another's name to real estate. A gift is considered to have been made when the new deed is issued.

If a parent and child are joint owners and one of them dies, the amount added to the decedent's estate is determined by who purchased and contributed to the holdings. It may thus be possible for all the holdings to be considered part of the estate of the first to die. If this is the child, both parents will become heirs.

Many people open a bank account in their own name together with a minor. For the most part, this is the creation of a joint account. There is confusion as to the proper method of taxing such an account. At least one court has held that interest earned on joint tenancies is taxable to the owners in proportion to their contribution. Another court has held that the contributions are immaterial and the taxes are to be on an equal basis. The IRS can be expected to take the position that such a joint account remains in the control of the adult.

Tax caution. An interesting point to consider is the use of Social Security numbers in opening joint accounts. Frequently, a lower-tax-paying grandmother will, without informing her child or grandchild, set up a joint account. The interest from that account is money that she expects to declare and pay taxes on at her lower bracket/rate. If the Social Security number of the child is listed first, however, the government may consider that the funds belong to the child, and an audit may be taken against an often unsuspecting child. To avoid this, be careful to list only the Social Security number of the person with the lower bracket/rate, or to list this number first. If actual divorce proceedings are pending, gifts may be suspended so the child is not "enriched," thus reducing the likelihood of a hearty child-support settlement.

The government permits a husband and wife each to give $10,000 per year tax-free and together they may give $20,000. Grandparents may give unlimited amounts to cover tuition or medical care costs without paying a gift tax. However, such payments must be made directly to the school or health care institution and such costs may not be covered by insurance.

The trust alternative. The donor who wishes to take advantage of income, gift, and estate tax savings may also wish to use a trust. It is possible to continue a trust beyond the child. The income from the trust may be distributed during the lifetimes of the grandchildren, then the great-grandchildren, then the great-great-grandchildren, and then, finally accrue to the great-great-great-grandchildren. Such an arrangement could allow wealth to pass tax-free through several generations. This came to a halt in 1976, with the imposition of a generation-skipping tax. Only a few trusts are subject to such a tax; most are not. The following criteria render the trust subject to taxation:

- The trust must have two or more beneficiaries.

- At least two of the beneficiaries must be from different generations (for example, child, grandchild).

- Each generation must be younger than that of the settlor (the one who established the trust).
  The tax on these trusts is the same whether they are *inter-vivos* or testamentary.

The following trusts are not subject to taxation:

- trusts to children only

- trusts to grandchildren only

- trusts to a spouse (that go to your child upon the death of the spouse)

- generation-skipping trust of less than $250,000

A special exclusion or exemption from this tax is available to grandparents. Transfers to grandchildren are not subject to the special tax if the total transfer does not exceed $250,000 for each transferor, the grandparent's own child being considered the transferor. Thus, a grantor-grandparent with two children could transfer $500,000 ($250,000 for each child) to the grandchildren tax-free.

Because of this high figure, most people will be able to create a generation-skipping trust. (It is unlikely that they will want to give more than $250,000 per child.) Nevertheless, even if it is $30,000 or $40,000 that they have in mind, be careful that their trusts meet all the eligibility rules for the grandchild exclusion. First of all, the property must actually be given to the child so that if the child dies the property becomes part of the child's estate. If there are contingencies regarding the child's going to school, getting married, or reaching a certain age, the exclusion is lost unless the grandchild has actually reached that age, performed the marriage, or fulfilled in some other way the stated contingency. If the trust exceeds $250,000, the exclusion applies until the *first* distribution in excess of $250,000 is made to a child. Make sure that the trustee understands this, so the first child to receive money does not use up all of the tax savings, leaving the other grandchildren to pay the tax.

Perhaps you would like to give gifts during your lifetime but can't afford to give up the income from the assets. This concept is discussed in the next Key.

34

GRITS—RETAINING AN INCOME FROM GIFTS YOU GIVE

Many people would like to transfer assets in excess of $600,000 to their heirs before their death. Doing so will help save taxes, and if placed in a trust, this action can also help in exercising some control over how the money is managed. As an added benefit, probate is avoided. Unfortunately, most people cannot take advantage of the benefits of a lifetime transfer to a trust because they need the income from the funds for day-to-day living.

There is an estate-planing technique that can help. The strategy consists of creating an irrevocable trust naming your beneficiaries as remaindermen (they are the ones who get the principal). You, the grantor, get the income for a period of years. The period's length depends on specific clauses in the trust and the rules under the Internal Revenue Code (IRC). In fact, these trusts are creatures of the IRC and their names are derived from the rules.

There are three types of irrevocable lifetime trusts that include features that permit the grantor to enjoy some use of the transferred assets, avoid probate, and also save estate taxes:

- GRITS (Grantor-Retained Income Trusts)

- GRATS (Grantor-Retained Annuity Trusts)

- GRUTS (Grantor-Retained Unitrusts).

Under a GRIT, the grantor retains an interest for a period of years, usually ten or fewer. If the grantor dies before that specified period expires, the trust value may be included in the estate but at less than its dollar value.

If the grantor outlives the period, the income from the assets stops. The gift is complete and is excluded from the estate. GRUTS and GRATS are more recent creatures of the Internal Revenue Code but they function similarly. If estate-tax planning is your goal, be sure to see a lawyer or financial planner familiar with these devices.

Under any of these alternatives, the grantor can continue to use the property in the trust (for example, continue to occupy a house) or collect the interest income for the investment of the sums.

In the next Key, special tax help for married couples is explored.

35

USING THE CREDIT-SHELTER TRUST AND MARITAL DEDUCTION TO REDUCE TAXES

As discussed in Key 26, all assets left to a spouse (without limitation) pass to that spouse free of federal estate tax. The only requirement is that the couple must be legally married at the time one of them dies and that there be very few restrictions on the survivor's use of the money. The issue of allowable restrictions will be investigated in the next Key.

For the many husbands and wives who wish to leave everything to each other, there need not be any federal estate tax in the first estate. But there's a problem! What happens in the second estate, when the survivor dies? Unless the survivor has been a spendthrift, has transferred money to other family members through gifts, or has had the cost of long-term health care, there may be a lot of money involved. Of course, if the spouse has remarried, the money can be left to the new spouse, free of federal estate tax. This occurs infrequently because the prenuptial agreement signed by both parties in a second marriage that waives inheritance rights is popular today.

Most often, the survivor leaves everything to the children of the first marriage. Without the marital deduction (which obviously does not apply when money is left to children), there is a stiff tax in the second estate. Because of the ever-increasing longevity of our people, the second estate can grow very large. For example, if Mom outlives Dad by twenty years, the estate can easily double, even if investments are simple and Mom lives well on the income.

There has been a new emphasis on protecting the second estate from taxes while planning the first estate. The most popular device is called the credit-shelter trust. Using it properly can save up to $192,500 in taxes and cost nothing. Because of the importance of this clause, everyone should recheck wills or trusts to be sure that such a clause exists. However, if all money is kept in joint accounts, the assets will not pass under the terms of the will or trust, even if there is such a clause. The most irritating thing for the estate attorney or financial planner is the existence of a nicely drafted credit-shelter trust that is useless because most of the couple's assets pass directly to each other through joint ownership. The following pointers present all you need to know to save up to $192,500:

Pointer Number One: *The object is to preserve the federal estate tax credit for the first person to die, which is wasted when all the assets are left outright to the spouse.*

You will recall that all of us as individuals have a lifetime exemption of assets from federal taxation of $600,000. This exemption is equivalent in dollars to a dollar-for-dollar tax credit of $192,500. If married, there also is an unlimited marital deduction. If everything is left to a spouse outright in a will, a trust, or a joint account, the credit is not needed or used and is wasted. It would be nice if it could be saved and used when the spouse dies. The second estate could then have up to $1,200,000 in exemption or double credit. But that's not the way the law works.

There is something, however, that you *can* do with good planning. You can leave everything except $600,000 to your spouse, and your will or trust could segregate funds for children or other heirs. Up to

$600,000 (the federal exemption) would apply and you would pay no tax. The rest of the money, left to your spouse outright, would also be tax-free by virtue of the marital deduction. This is a straightforward way of utilizing the $600,000 exemption or $192,500 credit. Here is an example:

- gross estate of husband = $800,000

- leave to children = $200,000 tax-free because Dad has up to $600,000 in exemption

- leave to wife = $600,000 tax-free under unlimited marital deduction

- Mom uses income from her money all her life but doesn't spend principal.

- Mom dies and leaves the principal of $600,000 to the children; her exemption applies to that amount and there is no tax to pay in her estate.

Now let's see what happens if Dad left all $800,000 to Mom. In his estate, the marital deduction would cancel any tax. But when Mom died, she would have $800,000 (or more if she only used the income from $600,000). Applying her $600,000 exemption, $200,000 is taxable. The tax on $200,000 is $74,000. By wasting Dad's exemption, the family unnecessarily paid taxes.

Pointer Number Two: *If you want your spouse to have the use of all your money, you can still take advantage of the credit if you use a credit-shelter trust in your will or living trust.*

As you read *Pointer Number One* you may have rejected the idea of giving a lot of money to your children outright while your spouse was still alive and able to enjoy and manage the money. There is a compromise between cutting the spouse out of the inheritance and wasting your tax credit. The compromise comes in the form of a clause that can be incorporated in a will or a trust. The clause is called a unified-credit clause, a credit-shelter clause, or a B trust (some lawyers have their own additional pet names). Using this clause preserves the tax credit but also allows the surviving spouse to have a lifetime income from the money.

Pointer Number Three: *Don't try this at home. Use the services of a professional.*

The one clause that is least adaptable to do-it-yourself trust and estate planning is the credit-shelter clause. This clause is designed to set up a trust that takes effect only at death (a testamentary trust). In it the executor named in the will or the trustee of the living trust creates an account in the name of the credit-shelter trust and distributes up to $600,000 of your assets to that trust. What does "up to" mean? The maximum is $600,000, but at the executor's or successor trustee's discretion, it can be less. This happens when the estate is small or the widow or widower acting as trustee or executor decides (after the spouse's death) not to take full advantage of the clause.

Once the trust has been established, the trustee takes over and administers it, invests the funds, and gives the income to the spouse, who is the income beneficiary. And when the spouse dies, the trustee distributes the principal to the children or other named beneficiaries.

Notice that while the executor of the will or successor trustee of the trust sets up the trust, neither one is usually the trustee who takes over and handles the trust throughout the years. Why? Because most of the time a competent spouse is named to take over the job of trustee of a living trust or to act as executor of the will if there is no living trust (see Key 4). But in most states, the spouse is prohibited from acting as trustee of the credit-shelter trust. In some states, the spouse can act as a co-trustee but not the sole trustee.

Pointer Number Four: *The credit-shelter trust has*

disadvantages for the spouse's freedom to use the money.

Because of the limitation on the spouse acting as trustee, there are restraints on the control of the spouse over the assets placed in the credit-shelter trust. The restraints vary from state to state, which is why an attorney must be used who is in practice in the state of residence of the spouse at the time the plan was created. For the most part, the surviving spouse is restricted to using only the income from the trust. If a *Crummey* power (see Key 32) is used, up to 5 percent of the principal can be withdrawn yearly. Finally, the trustee can invade the principal for health, education, or welfare. In that case, of course, this trust gives no protection against nursing-home or long-term care spend-down (see Key 30).

Many spouses would rather have free reign over all the funds and skip the credit-shelter trust, even though the trust saves taxes for the heirs. If this applies to you, see Key 40, in which the joint and survivor insurance policy is discussed. This can be an economical way to buy $192,500 in death benefits payable in the second estate. If you as a couple decide against the credit-shelter clause, you can make up for it by putting nonestate-taxable cash at the disposal of the estate when the survivor dies.

On the other hand, many spouses believe just the opposite. They want to restrict their spouses from the use of the money and still keep the marital deduction. A method of achieving spousal supervision is discussed in the next Key.

36

USING A QTIP TRUST TO REDUCE ESTATE TAXES

Often a spouse would like to place restrictions on the use of assets by another spouse, for reasons that are legion. Perhaps the spouse is incompetent and can't handle the investments. Perhaps a child puts undue pressure on a parent for money and the parent needs to be insulated. Perhaps the spouse believes there will be a second marriage and the survivor will not be diligent in keeping the money out of the hands of an existing second family. Perhaps the marriage is already a second marriage and the object is to protect the children of the first marriage while still saving taxes and giving access to funds to the second spouse. Yet under the rules of the unlimited marital deduction, the assets must pass directly to the spouse unfettered or they are ineligible and will be taxed in the first estate.

There is a way out of this dilemma—a QTIP trust. This acronym stands for "qualified terminable-interest property." Terminable-interest property is property that can only be used during one's lifetime. At the time of death, it goes to the heirs designated by the person who gave the gift, so the recipient has no right to determine who ultimately gets the property. Such restricted assets will not qualify for the marital deduction unless they are left by virtue of a will or a living trust to a QTIP trust.

Under the Internal Revenue code, a testamentary trust can be created designating the spouse as the lifetime beneficiary of income. At the time of the spouse's death, the money will go directly to the children, and the assets will be taxed in the second estate. To save taxes in that estate, the credit-shelter trust (Key 35) may be used or an insurance policy (Key 40) purchased.

The essence of the QTIP is:

- The surviving spouse has use of the income from the trust for life.

- The trustee can distribute the principal to the spouse for health, education, and welfare, along with support and maintenance where reasonable.

- The property should be in income-producing investments.

- The property is distributed as dictated in the trust when the surviving spouse dies.

- The trust funds pay the tax attributed to it in the estate of the second spouse (optional clause).

- The trust can have a *Crummey* clause (see Key 32).

In fact, the QTIP can even permit the spouse a limited power to decide who gets the principal or provide that the assets pour over into another trust (created on the death of the spouse) to be held for the children. This device is useful when the children are young or one has predeceased and there are young grandchildren involved. The trustees are usually the surviving spouse and an independent trustee jointly.

You will learn an entire model-estate plan for a married couple in Key 41. But first, let's look at another favored beneficiary, the charity.

37

USING CHARITABLE GIFTS TO REDUCE ESTATE TAXES

Uncle Sam has long supported the giving of private charitable gifts by providing substantial tax benefits to the donors. Most of us, however, believe that philantropy is only for the rich. Not true. The cynical among you won't be surprised to learn that the percent of income given is inversely proportional to the income of the donor. The fact is that the poor give a greater percentage of their income than do the rich. Yet, when the rich give, they do so in ways that benefit themselves as well. This Key should encourage giving by showing what the benefits are.

When you give to a charity, be sure it falls under the Internal Revenue Code's definition of a charity. Almost every legitimate cause will, including arts, medical research, schools, hospitals, religious institutions, and a lot more. Gifts to specific people for education and individual handouts do not qualify as charities, even if your heart is in the right place. If you hand out $50 or more during a year, you are better off making a one-time gift to a soup kitchen run as a not-for-profit corporation and getting a receipt. You can deduct the gift from your income tax in the year you gave it if you meet the rules. (See Key 38 for a discussion of income tax deductions and charitable gifts.)

No matter how much or little you give, you can check on a charity by getting in touch with National Charities Information Bureau, 19 Union Square West, New York, NY 10003-3395 and asking for a report.

You can also request Form 980 from the charity. To keep its tax-exempt status, the organization must file a yearly report showing how the money it receives is spent, how much goes to help the object of the charity, and how much goes to salaries and benefits for the staff. This type of investigation is particularly important if you are giving large gifts in order to save estate taxes.

If you have no specific charity in mind, you can use the services of the Community Trust, Two Park Avenue, New York, NY 10016, which researches charities and parcels out your gift among several with the same objective you have.

From an estate point of view, the charitable gift is an excellent planning tool. The rule is simple. Any amount of money you give to a qualified charity during your life or at your death is 100 percent free of gift and estate taxes. It doesn't matter whether or not you use a will or a trust or even donate funds while you are still alive. None of it is taxable. Charitable gifts are subtracted from your gross estate before it becomes your taxable estate (see Key 26). Before making any major plans, however, check with your tax professional. Congress frequently considers bills that limit the charitable deduction.

There are various types of assets you can give. Some individuals have given everything from insurance policies to cows. However, most charities are not prepared to accept certain types of gifts, and others have a planned-giving department that will help with estate planning and integrate the charitable gifts into the overall program. Some large charities will offer to prepare an estate plan free of charge if it includes a gift to them.

Charitable giving can be very important to a single person. Of course there are many spiritual and social aspects to giving. In addition, many charities are aware that with the new longevity, a large group of older people—statistically women—live alone, having outlived their loved ones. Pledging a gift can mean that the charity will help manage their money if they become disabled. Such an arrangement takes wise and thorough investigation but it can work wonders for a charity-minded person living alone.

A charity can also come in handy as a backup beneficiary. You may leave all your assets to an unmarried sister, but what if she predeceases you? A charity can be a successor beneficiary when you do not wish to benefit friends or family members.

Many would like to give charitable gifts but need the money for their own family. In the next Key, the creation of a win-win situation (by giving and getting at the same time, all with the help of the Internal Revenue Code) will be discussed.

38

USING CHARITABLE TRUSTS TO REDUCE ESTATE TAXES

For people who are charity-minded or who need some heavy strategic tax planning, there is no match for a charitable trust. The rules are not difficult, but people can be put off because the names are intimidating. To create a better image of the charitable trust, I will give you the official names of the rules, but use my made-up name for each of the three types. You should be familiar with all of them. I call them Hughie, Dewey, and Louie, after the three nephews of Scrooge McDuck of Disney cartoon fame. I'm certain that Mr. McDuck would not pass up the opportunity to use a charitable trust. Walt Disney himself might have done so, too.

The Hughie: Charitable Lead Trust. A Hughie can be set up while you are alive or created upon your death in accordance with the terms of your will or trust. If you set it up during your lifetime, it must be irrevocable and out of your control in order to qualify for tax benefits (see Key 29).

The Hughie provides that the income from the trust fund goes to a named charity. This can last for a specified number of years, until a specific event occurs, or until the death of a named individual. Upon the termination date, the remaining sum is distributed to a family member called the remainderman. If this sounds familiar, it should. It's just an irrevocable trust with a charity as income beneficiary instead of a person.

The Hughie has two benefits. First, of course, is the admirable purpose of giving income to charity for a period of years. The second is a tax purpose. Because the assets placed in the trust are being used to generate income for a charity, less than 100 percent of their value is counted in determining the gross estate for estate tax calculation. For example, if Dad left Son $50,000 in cash at his death, then that $50,000 is part of Dad's gross estate. If, however, a charity has the right to collect income on the money for a while, the $50,000 is discounted to a lesser sum before the taxable estate is calculated. This is true even though Son will eventually get the whole $50,000. The discount tables furnished by the Internal Revenue Service were more liberal in the past, but even today, an heir that does not need the money right away may end up with more after-tax dollars if a charity has the use of the money for a time. Naturally, your appointed trustee will oversee the investments and be sure that the principal remains intact. All the income goes to the charity until the designated period has elapsed.

The Dewey: Charitable Remainder Unitrust. The Dewey, which can also be set up as an irrevocable trust in your lifetime or as a testamentary trust in your will or *inter-vivos* trust, is just the opposite of the Hughie. Here the income beneficiary is not a charity but the remainderman *is* a charity. The income beneficiaries get the income from the trust for as long as they live and the trustee gives the principal to a named charity upon their deaths. This is particularly useful under these three circumstances:

1. You have an heir for whom you would like to provide a substantial lifetime income, but there is no one to whom you would like to leave a lump sum, after the demise of the income beneficiary.
2. You are a single person who wants steady income during your lifetime, but you don't want

to manage your money and there is no individual to whom you would like to leave an inheritance.

3. You have property that you would like to sell but doing so would incur a large capital gain, which you would like to avoid. You may or may not have an heir to whom you would like to leave the funds, but you would like to invest the cash from the sale in income-producing assets and use the income during your life.

If any of these scenarios apply to you, here is how the Dewey can help:

Case 1: Set up a Dewey in your will or trust. Name your heir as the income beneficiary for life and remainder to the charity. Provide that the executor or trustee transfer the assets prior to sale into the Dewey. Once the Dewey owns the assets, its trustee sells them. The capital gains tax is reduced (often to zero) because a charity and a charitable trust do not pay capital gains tax. Further, there is little estate tax on the assets since only the income goes to the noncharitable beneficiary.

For example, Mary purchased a blue chip stock for $10,000 in 1942. She died in 1990, when the asset was worth $100,000 and rising. She leaves an unmarried sister (who was never good at managing money) and no other heirs. The total of Mary's estate exceeds $600,000. She is in the 37 percent tax bracket and must consider state inheritance tax. Instead of giving the stock to her sister, Mary provides in her *inter-vivos* probate-avoiding trust that upon her death a testamentary trust be set up: a Dewey.

Sister is named the income beneficiary and Mary's favorite qualified charity is named remainderman. The charity's planned-giving service helps Mary choose a trustee, which is usually a lawyer who works for the charity, a professional trustee who works for many charities, or a charity-minded professional who acts as trustee free of charge to facilitate the planned-giving program.

The charity sells the stock at $110,000 (it rose $10,000 since Mary's death). It pays no capital gain. (The beneficiary would have paid a gain on $10,000; see Key 28.) The estate pays no estate tax. and saves at least 37 percent in taxes. The entire amount is invested by the charity and sums are paid out to Sister all her life. When she dies, the charity gets the remainder.

Under a Dewey, the amount paid out to Sister is a yearly percentage of at least 5 percent of the net fair market value of the total assets in the trust that year. Naturally, with a good money manager for the trust, Sister's yearly income is greater than it would be with one who is inept. Mary, therefore, in choosing the charity, must research its past investment performance with trusts. In any case, Sister is deriving income from at least 37 percent more money than if she inherited the asset directly.

Case 2: You set up a Dewey during your lifetime as you would any irrevocable trust. You are the income beneficiary for your lifetime. At your death the charity gets the remainder. In so doing, you get a triple tax benefit. First, when you transfer the assets to the Dewey, you get a charitable deduction from your income tax. The deduction can be carried over to another tax year if you don't need the entire deduction the year in which you make the gift. If you transfer a large sum, you may not have to pay income taxes for years. Second, the charity (not you) sells the asset so there is no capital gain, thereby leaving more to invest for your lifetime income. Third, upon your death the money is out of your estate and free of estate taxes. The charity gets a handsome sum and your memory gets a handsome plaque.

For example, Mary has $100,000 worth of stock for which she originally paid $10,000 in 1942. She lives alone, has no heirs, and needs more income. Mary is told by her accountant that if she sold the stock she would have to pay a capital gains tax of approximately $25,000 (actual figures are a bit higher). Income from the reinvested $75,000 gives Mary $4,500 a year if she invests at 6 percent. With a Dewey, Mary gets 5 percent of the total annual net assets in the trust. With no tax upon the sale of the stock to the trust, Mary is working with a $100,000 base.

Let's say the trustee invested the funds at the same 6 percent. By the end of the first year, the assets are $105,000 (with a fee deducted for the trustee). Mary gets 5 percent under the terms of the Dewey—that's $5,250. In addition, Mary has such a big tax deduction that she may pay no income tax that year, whereas the alternate return of $4,500 would be entirely taxable.

Case 3: All this sounds good, but what if Mary is a widow with children to whom she wishes to leave a legacy? The strategy is to have Mary purchase an insurance policy equal to the amount she puts in trust, then name an irrevocable life insurance trust as owner. Her children are named as the beneficiaries of the trust and will receive the death benefit (tax-free) upon her death. The charity receives the assets in the Dewey free of tax.

For example, Mary is a 60-year-old widow with two adult children and three grandchildren. She has a taxable estate including $100,000 in stock for which she paid $10,000 in 1942. She anticipates, however, that she will need more income because of inflation. Mary creates a Dewey during her lifetime and names herself as beneficiary of income and the charity of her choice as remainderman. She gets the tax benefits and income as described above (Case 2).

She also buys a life insurance policy, using some of the extra income for the premium, or perhaps the kids chip in to pay the premium. The life insurance trust assures that the death benefit goes to the children, estate-tax free (see Key 39).

As long as the death benefit exceeds $48,000, the family is ahead of the game. Here's why: If Mary sold the stock herself she would end up with $75,000 (after taxes) to invest for income (see Case 2 for that calculation). Mary then uses all the income and leaves the $75,000 to the children. But first her estate pays an estate tax of at least 37 percent, reducing the actual inheritance to about $48,000.

Some people, however, would prefer a definite amount of income instead of a percentage of the trust's net asset value. In that case, they want a Louie.

The Louie: Charitable Remainder Annuity Trust. This is precisely like the Dewey, except for the way the income paid to the income beneficiary is calculated. The amount for a Louie is never less than 5 percent of the initial fair market value of the asset when transferred to the trust; in Mary's case, 5 percent of $100,000, or $5,000. If investment management isn't so good, the income beneficiary gets the minimum figure. But even with the best planning, taxes must often be paid. In the next Key, we will describe an economical way to secure payment.

39

USING INSURANCE TRUSTS TO PAY ESTATE TAXES

Possibly the insurance policy was the first financial product ever created. Banned by the Church in the 19th century as gambling, today it is the mainstay of most estate-planning programs and, ironically, an important way to give a lasting gift to the church or other charity. The right policy, properly used, is the single most important tool in reducing and building an estate. Here's how to use it.

First, work out a plan with your attorney and/or accountant to reduce your taxes through the other methods described in this book. Once you have a fair idea of the amount of tax your estate may have to pay (if calculated at its present value), you are ready to use insurance for paying Uncle Sam with pennies on the dollar.

Have your accountant, your computer, or your own pencil recalculate the tax as if it were the estimated date of your death. Right now the average person can use 84. If you live to that age (statistically, you will live longer) and your assets are growing at a rate of 6 percent a year after taxes, you can calculate how much tax you will be paying in the years ahead. This is very important. Most lawyers and even accountants don't take the growth value of your estate into consideration when giving you an idea of your estate tax exposure.

Every computer software program on estate planning, however, includes such projected calculations. The most avid purchasers of such software are insurance salespeople, who want you to see the full extent of your tax exposure. Certainly, it's a selling tool, but it's also the right way to determine what the true figure will be. If you have no attorney or accountant helping you, or if their fees to calculate are too high, by all means get a free projection from an insurance company. You'll know right away if the company really understands estate planning. If so, it will probably make a sale and you will get a lot of free professional help.

This calculation will help you determine how much insurance to buy. Shop for the policy from a high-rated company. Check Best's, Standard & Poor's, and Weiser's ratings, books that are available in the reference section of your library. Agents will also give you the ratings of their companies.

Once you have selected the policy, complete the application. Be sure to indicate that the trust (for example, "The Jenny Jones Life Insurance Trust") is the owner of the policy. When asked for the tax number, write "tax identification number pending." The trustee of your life insurance trust must be named and must also sign the application.

When you have passed the physical examination and the policy can be issued, see your lawyer immediately. The trust must be in existence and signed when the policy is issued.

If there is no existing trust, the policy will be issued to you as owner and you can transfer it to the trust when it has been created. The problem with that procedure is that under the Internal Revenue Code, if you die within three years of the transfer, the insurance proceeds are taxed in your estate. If the policy is issued directly to a trust, the proceeds are not counted and are paid to the trust, and eventually to the heirs, tax-free. Why? Because you don't own or control the policy at your death—the trustee does (see Key 29).

Therefore, to keep the proceeds of any life insurance policy entirely tax-free, either be sure that the trust owns it from its issue date, or have it transfered to the trust as soon as possible and outlive the three-year limitation.

Why not just make your heirs the owner right away? Why bother with a life insurance trust?

1. With a trust, you can give the trustee the power to lend money tax-free to your estate. The estate will then have liquid dollars to pay the tax within nine months of your death, as required by the IRC. If you gave the money directly to your heirs, there are no guarantees that they will use the proceeds to pay taxes. If you have more than one heir, each may want to take a different and conflicting approach.

2. Although your heirs will own the policy, you should pay for it each year. If you give them the premium, it is a gift. They can decide not to use the money for insurance and even let the policy lapse. So much for good planning.

3. If you pay the premiums directly and your heirs own the policy, the Internal Revenue Service may argue that you still have control over the policy and try to count the proceeds in your gross estate.

4. If you have a trust, you can use the now famous *Crummey* powers. (Named after a 1968 9th Circuit Federal Court case, this clause gets a special treatment in Key 32.) In an insurance trust, it allows you to transfer a yearly sum to the trust equal to the premium and have the trustee use it to pay the premium. The amount (up to $10,000 per beneficiary) is tax-excluded under the gift rules.

Your attorney will know the rules for a proper trust. And of course you will advise in the matter of provid-

ing for the distribution of any proceeds th;
used to pay taxes.

The final concern is to make sure that the d
efit is kept out of your estate. Here are some precau-
tionary things you can do to prevent the IRS from
including the money in the estate.

1. Keep more than just the bare amount of the premium in the trust.
2. Contribute a sum that is not the same as the premium each year.
3. Don't require the trustee to pay premiums. Just give the power to do so.
4. Use a professional trustee if possible.
5. Don't time the contributions to the trust with the date a premium payment is due.

If you are creating an irrevocable trust for other reasons, you can use it as an insurance trust as well. You need not have two trusts as long as the trustees' powers include lending to the estate.

In the next Key, a new type of insurance policy is introduced that can further reduce taxes.

40

PAYING TAXES WITH TEN CENTS ON THE DOLLAR

A particular type of life insurance has been gaining favor. The product is alternatively called "joint and survivor" and "second to die." A policy is taken on the measuring lives of a husband and wife or of business partners. No death benefit is paid until both measuring lives have expired. In other words, both spouses or both partners must die before the beneficiaries collect. This provision makes the policy most useful for heirs who, after the demise of their surviving parent, must pay a tax. If the family fortune is tied up in real estate, a family business, or other hard-to-liquidate assets, a death benefit coming at this time can mean the difference between good planning and disaster. But timing is not the only benefit of this type of policy.

Most notably, because it is based on two lives, the cost is substantially lower than two separate policies. It is also usually lower than one policy written on one life. For example, a 60-year-old male in good health who never smoked might pay roughly $31,470 a year in premiums for a $1,000,000 policy. A female under the same circumstances would pay $25,200. If they took a joint policy it would cost $36,066. Moreover, many husbands and wives are not the same age. Having a younger spouse provides many benefits, not the least of which is cheaper insurance. A 50-year-old wife with a 60-year-old husband would pay $33,960 for a million dollars in death benefit.

In addition, the medical underwriting requirements

are usually more lenient, and an uninsurable person is often given a policy in a joint-and-survivor application. The policy is also available to people of more advanced ages than is the usual whole life policy. As the couple ages and their estate grows, they may find for the first time that there is a high level of taxation. If all other planning avenues are exhausted, they may be able to buy a policy even in their 80s.

For the most part, the second-to-die policies should be issued to an insurance trust as owner (see Key 39 for an explanation of the insurance trust). The heirs are beneficiaries and trustees. The powers clause will give the trustees the right to lend the death benefit to the estate of the deceased in order to pay taxes, the usual arrangement for an insurance trust. While the husband and wife are alive, the policy will be gaining cash value. The powers can permit a *Crummey* withdrawal (Key 32) for the benefit of the couple. They can also permit the couple to borrow out of cash value.

In buying these policies there are many consumer awareness points. Most are matters of common sense, but others are technical.

1. These policies are a combination of term insurance and whole life. You can design the proportion with your insurance agent. The greater the percentage of term, the cheaper the policy, but the less you will accumulate in cash value. Most people with high tax liabilities prefer lesser premiums rather than more cash. Be aware, however, that term costs do increase with age.

2. Many joint and survivor policies allow conversion to a single policy if there is a divorce.

3. Costs of the policy vary widely. Shop for this type of insurance as you would any kind of insurance.

4. Some companies start out with a low premium that doubles after several years, but they claim

that the accumulated dividends will be enough to cover the additional cost. Carefully check their dividend's past performance.

5. Check the quality and safety of the company with reference books from Best, Moody, or Standard & Poor's. A little known company, Weiser, also rates many insurance companies. Also, an insurance company will usually provide its ratings on request. Your library reference section will contain copies of the publications noted above.

6. Discuss the possibility of the premium "vanishing" in a certain number of years. Most companies will have you pay more up front so the premiums are covered in later years by the dividends. By paying more earlier, more dividends will accumulate. But once again, be aware that all dividends are mere projections. Usually, no more than four percent is guaranteed.

Under the right circumstances, these policies will not only pay taxes, but will also help you build a substantial estate for your heirs in a most economical way. Every couple and business entity should explore its use.

In the next two Keys, we will see how to put many of the preceding concepts into practice.

41

COMBINING STRATEGIES—MARRIED PEOPLE

Sam and Janet Evening are a happily married couple. They have three adult children. Their son Early has two children of his own, Starry and Moonlit. Their younger daughter Late is not yet married and intends to complete medical school. Their elder daughter Summer is a bit of a drifter. She has been married several times and has one child, Wilde Evening, who is 15 and aspires to be a stockbroker.

Sam and Janet have assets of $1,500,000 as follows:

- a $400,000 home for which they paid $75,000, which has no mortgage;
- a $250,000 whole life death benefit on Sam's life, owned by Sam with Janet named as beneficiary;
- $250,000 in Sam's retirement account with Janet named as beneficiary;
- $100,000 in joint named bank certificates of deposit (CDs);
- $150,000 in Janet's pension plan with Sam named as beneficiary;
- $50,000 in furniture, art, and jewelry; and
- $300,000 in municipal bonds that Janet's mother gifted to Janet before she went into a nursing home.

At present, Sam and Janet have wills leaving everything to each other. After both die, everything is left equally to the children. If one of the children predeceases them, that child's share goes to his or her heirs "per stirpes." Sam and Janet aren't quite sure what "per stirpes" means, but they were so anxious to get the will completed that they let it go. What's wrong with this plan? Let me count the mistakes.

1. The family is overpaying in taxes. By today's standards they will pay federal taxes of approximately $351,000, plus any taxes imposed by the state in which they live. Simple planning would reduce the tax to $102,000.

2. They are not taking inflation and growth into account. The actual eventual tax could be double that amount if they invest well.

3. The have given no thought to the different financial needs and temperaments of their children and grandchildren.

4. They have given no thought to the possibility of their incapacity.

5. They have given no thought to the possibility of avoiding probate.

6. They could have done better emotionally and financially by Janet's mother.

First, let's correct their tax mistakes. Remember that this example is tailored to explain the situation easily to you. No doubt a tax lawyer or accounting professional would do an even better (certainly a more comprehensive) job of saving taxes for the couple, but here is the tax situation if we do no further planning.

If Sam dies first, Janet will inherit everything (either under the will or by designation of beneficiary) including insurance and pension, and (because she is joint owner), the certificates of deposit and the house (see Keys 8, 9, and 10). There will be no tax whatsoever because of the unlimited marital deduction. This is true even if the assets are greatly increased by the time Sam dies. If Janet dies first, there will also be no tax for the reasons stated above. (See Key 35 for an explanation of the unlimited marital deduction.)

In the second estate, the tax picture is far less rosy. If Janet dies after Sam, her total estate is worth $1,500,000, assuming that there is no growth in the assets and Janet spent all the income from the assets while she was alive. Janet would apply her $600,000 exemption and there would be a tax on $900,000. The federal tax alone is $351,000. The state tax would vary depending on the state that Janet resided in at the time of her death. If there was even a 4 percent yearly gain on the assets and Janet outlived her husband by five years the tax on her estate would be $473,464.

Now let's look at four ways that good planning, using the techniques you have already learned, can save a fortune in taxes.

1. Both Sam and Janet should have a credit-shelter trust clause in their wills (see Key 35). Under this clause, when the first spouse dies, up to $600,000 of his or her assets are placed in trust. The surviving spouse gets the income from the assets for life. Also under the *Crummey* provision, up to $5000 or 5 percent of the trust funds can be withdrawn each year if desired (see Key 32). Further, the trustee (usually an adult child and in Sam and Janet's case, probably son Early and daughter Late jointly) can also use the money for the parent's health, welfare, and other needs. The children get the principal that remains when the surviving parent dies. The credit shelter trust assures that both parent's lifetime $600,000 exemption is used.

However, both Sam and Janet must have at least $600,000 in their names at the time of their deaths to fund the trust, so ownership of their assets would have to be arranged during their lifetime. One way to accomplish this would be to:

- leave the house ownership as it is so Sam and Janet will avoid probate and taxes in the first estate;
- divide the CDs equally into one account of $50,000

121

for Janet and one account for $50,000 for Sam;

- leave Janet with the $300,000 of municipal bonds in her own name to avoid family friction (because it belonged to her mother);
- call the $50,000 in miscellaneous property equally owned by both of them (to avoid IRS problems);
- change the designation of beneficiary on Janet's pension to read one-half to Sam and one-half to Janet's estate;
- change the beneficiaries of Sam's pension to one-half to Janet and one-half to Sam's estate; and
- change the beneficiary of the insurance policy to give $25,000 to Janet and $225,000 to Sam's estate.

If you add up the new asset configuration, you'll see that Sam has $575,000 in his name and Janet $525,000, plus joint ownership of the marital home.

The sums in their name alone will go into the credit-shelter trust for the lifetime benefit of the surviving spouse. The remainder will either already be in the ownership of the survivor or pass to the survivor by designation of beneficiary. When the second one goes, much of the $600,000 credit of the other will have been utilized. The surviving spouse will leave only the remainder to the children, after subtracting the balance of the credit. Total federal tax is $102,000 as compared to $351,000. If there is inflation or growth, the numbers are adjusted accordingly.

Why not divide up the estate to take full advantage of the $600,000? That could be done, but sometimes it's better to do the emotionally correct thing than it is to save taxes.

Here are three more strategies that could reduce taxes further:

1. The couple can gift away some of the assets they don't think they will need. The couple can give up to $120,000 each year to their six beneficiaries

as an additional tax-free transfer ($20,000 per year per beneficiary as a split gift) (see Key 31).

2. They can use a GRIT, GRAT, or GRUT (see Key 34) to gift assets to an irrevocable trust and still keep income for themselves for a period of time.

3. They can buy a joint and survivor policy providing a premium of $100,000 to pay the taxes with discounted dollars (see Key 40).

Now that we've saved the family approximately a quarter of a million dollars ($351,000 − $102,000), let's solve their other problems. Happily, many objectives can be met with the revocable trust. They can use the trust instead of a will to avoid probate. Each spouse would have an individual trust containing a credit-shelter trust. Instead of naming the estate as beneficiary in dividing up assets, they would designate the revocable trust to receive the assets upon death. They can also put a clause in the trust giving the other a power-of-attorney in the case of incapacity (see Key 23).

In either a trust or a will, they can give thought to the ultimate distribution of the assets to the children. The assets can be divided into thirds but the flighty Summer's share could be left in trust. The grandchildren could have money left to them equally instead of dividing their parent's share. The doctor-to-be daughter could be given money for medical school while the parents are alive and this sum could be mentioned in the trust as an advance against her inheritance, to be fair to the other children.

As for Grandma, instead of taking her $300,000 outright, the sum could have been placed in a trust with Janet as the trustee. Grandma could receive only a limited income right (the amount that the state allows a Medicaid beneficiary to keep for sundries). Upon Grandma's death, the money could go to Janet or it could skip a generation and save any taxation for a long period of time (see Key 33.)

42

COMBINING STRATEGIES—SINGLE PEOPLE

While all unmarried people are in different situations and have various and differing wishes concerning their estates, there are several points of common interest. They include:

- avoiding probate

- saving estate taxes in the absence of the marital deduction

- naming a beneficiary

- naming a fiduciary

Here is a roundup of some of the planning ideas that have been discussed in many of the preceding Keys. All of them have a special significance for the single person who is involved in estate planning for the future.

Avoid probate with a revocable trust. This will solve not only the probate problem, but also allow the single person to include a durable power-of-attorney and name a trustee to handle funds in the event of incompetency. An individual who is not married may want to record the revocable trust in the county of residence, surrogate clerk's office. This is appropriate if the single person has only remote heirs who are not likely to know where personal papers are.

Many singles are concerned with continuing care in the event of a lengthy illness during their lifetime. The revocable trust permits instructions to fiduciaries and beneficiaries that can be changed at the single's discretion, but that will avoid a conservatorship proceeding to determine how money should be expended in the event of illness.

Save estate taxes and get more lifetime income from charitable giving. If choosing a beneficiary is your problem, consider a charity for several reasons:

1. It is unmatched for the spiritual and psychic rewards it provides.
2. It brings you into a caring community and in some cases may even provide the fiduciary help you need.
3. It eliminates estate tax because of favored treatment.
4. If your assets have appreciated, you can transfer them as a charitable gift in trust. The charity will liquidate them, pay no tax, and invest the entire sum for you. You will get income as long as you live, and upon your death, the charity will inherit the principal.
5. If you have heirs, you can make a charitable gift as outlined in 4 above and replace their inheritance with a tax-free insurance policy. In this way, you can pass on the estate to your heirs tax-free, get a charitable tax deduction from your income tax while you live, and also maximize your income-producing investments by avoiding capital gains on the sale of non-income-producing assets (the charity will sell them for you as part of the charitable trust).

    Often the tax deduction and the extra income from investing the untaxed dollars results in a saving larger than the cost of the replacement insurance.

Talk to your heirs. Tell them your wishes, write a health-care instruction document, execute organ-donor cards, and select a burial site (also including instructions in your will or trust). No one knows what you have in mind for your heirs or what your desires are unless you tell them.

Make friends with a large, ongoing professional firm. Your banker, attorney, or accountant may be your best fiduciary. But individual professionals change their affiliations, move on, retire, and die. You will want to choose individuals within an organization that will be ongoing even after specific people are gone. Your relationship with the group can last for years.

The past several Keys have presented a lot for you to think about. But even if your planning wasn't perfect, there are things that your family can do after your death in order to save taxes. You'll learn more about this aspect of estate planning and about post mortem planning in the next Key.

43

DISCLAIMERS AND POST MORTEM PLANNING

It might seem that with all the planning alternatives available during a lifetime, it's too late to do much more after death. On the contrary, some essential estate-planning and tax-saving tools are available only upon demise. They are exercised by the heirs, but the decedent is the one that made the planning possible and prepared the way.

An example is the "disclaimer," also called a "renunciation." This is a procedure in which a beneficiary refuses a bequest. In that case, the bequest lapses and the other heirs named in the will or trust get the money. If no preparation has been done and no other heirs are named, the funds will be distributed in accordance with the laws of the state of residence of the decedent at the time of death.

It may seem foolish for anyone to refuse a bequest, but in some cases there is a good tax reason. Let's say Mr. and Mrs. Bridge make a will leaving everything to each other. The will does not contain a credit-shelter trust as explained in Key 35, so the $600,000 credit is wasted in the estate of the first spouse to die. In 1955, when the Bridges made their will, they never dreamed that they would accumulate a lot of wealth. They also never revised their wills.

After forty years of marriage, Mr. Bridge dies. He's content to know that everything goes to his beloved wife. But Mrs. Bridge is about his age. She realizes that upon her death the children will have to pay a large estate tax and will only have the use of her $600,000 exemption. She also believes that she doesn't need all the income from all the assets in order to live well.

Mrs. Bridge can decide to renounce all or part of her inheritance. If she renounces $600,000, that amount will go to the children directly from Dad's estate. His $600,000 exemption will apply and no tax will be paid. When Mrs. Bridge dies, her exemption will be used. With this plan, neither parent will have wasted their exemption/credit.

During Mr. Bridge's lifetime, he could have prepared for a disclaimer by placing a clause in his will or trust that stated who would get the money in the event that Mrs. Bridge disclaims. He could even have named a trust for the children or for Mrs. Bridge herself. In this way, he could have left everything to his wife and, if (at her discretion) it is better not to inherit it all, his wishes would apply to its distribution.

For a disclaimer to be effective, it must be in writing and irrevocable, and it must conform to both federal and state law. One essential federal requirement is that the disclaimer be made within nine months after the date of death.

Another important post mortem decision involves pension proceeds and 401(k) and IRA plans. Often the decedent has not withdrawn all the funds prior to death. The heirs have various options depending on the program. They usually can withdraw all the funds, pay the estate tax, and terminate the plan. Or they can be substituted as the plan owners and their lifespans (as determined by actuarial tables) applied to create a lifetime annuity that will liquidate the fund by the time they die. They will receive monthly income for life and pay taxes over time. A third possibility is to use a joint life (surviving spouse and a child) insurance policy to determine the actuarial life span. This reduces the amount of each monthly payment, but payments continue over a longer period of time.

If you are the beneficiary of a pension plan and the person dies, you must work with the professionals to decide post mortem. First, have an accounting professional calculate the tax consequences of each choice. Then meet with a financial advisor to see what you would do with the money if you took it in a lump sum. Finally, look back over the investment record of the pension plan and judge how you liked the service and investment strategy over the years. You must decide what to do based on the tax consequences and the likely investment performance of the funds in your hands as compared to the annuity.

A third category of post mortem planning also deals with an annuity, but in an entirely different context. If you have an adult child who cannot handle funds, you would most likely want to create a trust. Sometimes the estate is too small to warrant a paid trustee and there is no relative to act as trustee. Or perhaps there is an older relative who can serve, but no successor if that person must step down for health reasons. In such a case, one solution is to authorize the executor or trustee to use estate assets to purchase a lifetime annuity for the adult child.

A lifetime annuity is purchased through an insurance company. That is a contract under which (in return for giving the company a lump sum of money) a monthly amount will be paid to a named beneficiary for life. The monthly amount is guaranteed and calculated when the contract is made. It varies with the age and sex of the beneficiary and amount of lump sum given in each case. A $25,000 life annuity for a 40-year-old will provide much less monthly income than for a 60-year-old. But presumably, payments will be made over a longer period of time. Because the monthly payment is both interest and a return of principal, a percentage of it is tax free.

You can give your executor or trustee power to buy such an annuity and put the asset on automatic pilot. Even with no ongoing trust, the beneficiary's money is managed and doled out. Many companies guarantee that even if the beneficiary lives a short life, it will continue to pay at least the principal back or pay for a minimum of ten years. The will or trust should name a successor beneficiary in case the incompetent adult lives only a short time.

A final post mortem decision determines how taxes should be paid. It is probably best to decide this yourself and you can do so by giving specific directions in your will or trust. For example, a clause can state that the tax attributed to a particular bequest be paid out of that bequest, not out of the estate in general. Remember that if there is property passing outside of a will or trust, you can refer to it in the document and designate from which funds taxes attributed to it should be paid. This is very important in divorce settlements. Dad may have set aside a joint account for a first family under the terms of an agreement and left everything by will to the second family. But if no provisions are made, the second family will pay the tax attributed to the joint account.

In the next Key, we will discuss how these and other decisions are calculated on the actual tax form.

44

THE 706 FORM—ESTATE TAX FILING

Even though you may have successfully structured your estate to avoid probate, you must still file the federal estate tax return. Some estates are exempt from filing because they are under the $600,000 limit. Others must file a state tax form but no federal form. If you have set up joint or payable-on-death accounts, the bank or brokerage house will request a tax waiver form (showing that the estate is either not taxable or that all taxes are paid) before it releases the asset.

All of these forms and filings should be taken care of by an accountant. One difficulty occurs in determining whether the professional is fully familiar with the tax laws in this area. To judge more effectively, here are some of the rules that will enable you to ask the right questions:

1. Returns are due nine months after death unless an extension is granted by the IRS. The late filing of a return without cause subjects the estate to a handsome penalty. Penalty amounts change but specialists will know the amount.

2. The fiduciary requests the extension, which is easily granted for a six-month period.

3. Tax is due nine months after the date of death. It can be paid in cash or by redeeming U.S. government bonds called flower bonds. They have a special estate feature: even if they have not yet matured when the owner dies, the maturity date is accelerated to date of death, if used to pay

estate taxes. Flower bonds are difficult to get today but many people still have them in their portfolios.

4. The IRS often grants an extension up to twelve months from the due date. With hardship and reasonable cause, deferrals of up to ten years are possible.

5 Where a major asset is a family business, up to fifteen years deferral can be arranged (see Key 47).

6. Almost all deferrals require that interest be paid to the IRS on the unpaid tax.

7. The executor is personally liable for the tax. If an extension for family business is elected, the lien procedure can be used so that the executor is not liable throughout several years.

8. The executor's personal liability may be limited to one year from the date of filing, if a request for prompt audit and release of personal liability is made.

While the tax aspects of estate planning are for everyone, the next Key is of particular interest to individuals entering second marriages, divorcing, or adopting a child.

45

THE REALITIES OF DIVORCE, REMARRIAGE, AND ADOPTIONS

Blended families, extended families, single-parent families, and weekend visitations are part of our present family structures. Fluidity is the rule, not the exception. Even the so-called nuclear family (husband, wife, and 2.3 children) may be subject to possible changes in the future. A frequently asked question is from parents who want to know how to give a wedding gift or inheritance to their child that will be protected if there is a divorce.

The estate-planning rules have developed piecemeal, but there is a potpourri of tidbits of information that will keep you on the right track. Let's look at what you should know.

To limit the rights of a former spouse — Remember that a surviving spouse has an elective right to one-third of your property in most states, one-half in community property states, and a court-adjudicated fraction in the few remaining jurisdictions. If you have separated in your hearts, minds, and living arrangements, this is not good enough. Your estranged spouse is still entitled to a share, called an elective share, which can be sought in court despite the provisions of a will or trust to the contrary.

Moreover, in many states there is a month or more cooling-off period where even after a valid divorce, the spouse has an entitlement. In those states that permit no-fault divorce based on the signing of a separation agreement, one year usually elapses between signing and the actual divorce. The soon-to-be ex-spouse still has rights.

It may be a surprise to learn that if a spouse dies during a divorce proceeding, some states allow relatives to posthumously carry on the proceedings. Some states, however, do not and the surviving spouse gets a statutory windfall. Remember, too, that the length of the marriage, which has a great deal to do with alimony and property settlements while the parties are alive, has nothing to do with inheritance rights. A marriage of a day gives the same spousal rights as a marriage of fifty years.

Finally, in most states a divorce doesn't automatically revoke a prior will. In some states (like New York) the provision regarding an ex-spouse is revoked if the will was made during the marriage and not changed after the divorce. The spousal share usually falls into the residuary clause, a catchall clause that often names the spouse and children. Much confusion can arise. If an ex-spouse was named trustee or executor, that provision is automatically revoked by a divorce in most states. The successor then serves.

Caveat: While your will may be amended by a divorce insofar as it names the former spouse as beneficiary, your designation of that individual as beneficiary on insurance policies, joint accounts, and pensions will remain in full force and effect. The ex-spouse will get the money.

Luckily, if any of the above rules do not suit you, there is something simple you can do. You can take care of it all by negotiating a separation or divorce clause that waives the rights to inheritance by your soon-to-be ex-spouse. You can then make a new will that gives the money to the heirs of your choice. Even if you have to give up something to negotiate an acceptable clause, it is well worth it. It may be the only way to protect a second family or even the children of the first marriage.

To protect the children of a first marriage — It is never easy for second spouses to accept obligations to a first family. This is particularly true if they don't have reciprocal duties to theirs. Yet most of the wealth may have been accumulated during the first marriage. There may be adult or even small children to protect. A widow or widower may want to respect the wishes of a first spouse regarding how the money should be allocated. For all of these reasons, a second spouse's inheritance rights may need to be limited.

The fact is that the very act of remarriage gives the second spouse the elective right to a statutory share, iron clad, no matter how short that marriage turns out to be. What's more, in many states a remarriage revokes any prior will that may have been made. There is chaos afoot.

Once again, however, there is a remedy. Only the emotions and concerns over the effect on the new relationship will limit the manner in which the situation is approached. Here are options:

1. Insist on a prenuptial agreement. Make it fair, be sure that full disclosure takes place and make sure that the spouse-to-be is separately represented by council. This agreement will supersede all the state statutes if correctly drawn.
2. Make a joint or contractual will with a second spouse. This option is not very popular with lawyers because it limits freedom to change one's mind, but it is sometimes the right device. Under a separate contract accompanying a will or by virtue of joint-will language, each spouse agrees to leave money to the other's children or heirs. The will cannot be unilaterally changed and the survivor must abide by its terms. If the survivor makes a contrary will, the first family can contest and usually win.
3. Life estates and life leases can be given to a second spouse in the marital home with the first

family inheriting the property. In this way, the children get the real estate but cannot evict the surviving second spouse.

4. Do not simply give all your money away to the first family without the consent of the second spouse. In some states (like Wisconsin) this is against statutory law. In other states (like Florida), it is a fraud against the marriage and can be set aside.

5. Give the second spouse the required one-third share but do it through a QTIP trust (see Key 36). This will fulfill the spousal elective share but keep the principal intact for the children of the first marriage. It can also be done without the consent of the second spouse.

To protect adopted children — Once legally adopted, most states include a child in the generic references "heirs," "children," and the like. If there is no legal adoption but a child is supported or acknowledged and later is cut out, contesting the will can be successful. If a nonadopted child (a foster or stepchild) is included, make explicit provisions in your will or trust. Sometimes children of a first family are made heirs by will or trust while children of a second family are named beneficiaries of a life insurance policy or vice versa. These options depend on the family relationship, hostilities, and sensibilities.

To protect gifts to children and grandchildren in the event of divorce — The gifts and inheritances received from relatives during a valid marriage are not counted as marital property. This is a relief to many parents of adult children in a rocky marriage. However, the potential or actual wealth is considered by the court in fairly awarding child support and alimony (today called maintenance in many states).

To protect from any inclusion in a court's consideration is difficult. It is possible only if the child keeps the gift completely separate from all marital funds and never comingles the proceeds, or the funds are left in a trust that terminates in the event of a divorce. The funds will then be distributed to a sibling or other beneficiary. These are difficult approaches to take "just in case." But some children already have a record of wasting family inheritance and gifts through bad relationships.

Grandchildren are easily protected if given their inheritance in a minor's trust. However, be sure to name the child, not both parents, as trustee. If the parent of the child dies, name a successor trustee other than the surviving parent.

These items may not be of equal importance to everyone, but what does usually get attention are the rules relating to your home or primary residence. See the next Key for a discussion.

46

GIFTING THE HOME AND SAVING ESTATE TAXES

When it comes to your primary residence, you are most likely planning for your most important asset. There are a number of estate strategies relating to your home that can solve special problems and create the best package of tax savings, financial security, and distribution to your heirs. Because this is a very individual and sometimes emotional topic, the most important tax and distribution facts are listed here for your use.

1. *Stepped-up Basis.* Perhaps the most important concept in structuring the estate plan regarding a residence is understanding the stepped-up basis rule of the Internal Revenue Code. Under this rule, all property inherited is valued for estate-tax purposes at the fair market value at the date of death or six months thereafter. The executor or trustee decides whether to choose the date-of-death value or the six-month value, but the choice must be consistent for all assets (for a general discussion, see Key 28).

Under the rule, the heir of a home is deemed to have the date-of-death/six-month value as the basis. If the heir sells the property, the profit is calculated on the amount in excess of the date-of-death/six-month value. By contrast, if a gift of a home (or any other asset) is given during the donor's lifetime, the donee must use the donor's basis (the price the donor paid for the asset plus the cost of purchase and improvements).

The difference between leaving a home in a will or trust and giving it during your lifetime has a profound effect on the family fortune. For example, if a home was purchased at a price of $25,000 in 1955 and is worth $150,000 today, the heir who inherits will get the stepped-up $150,000 basis. Upon sale, taxes will be owned only upon the difference between the sale price and the date-of-death value/six-month value. If the property was transferred through a lifetime gift, the tax would be on the difference between $25,000 and the sale price.

For this reason, a homeowner must be very cautious about making a lifetime gift of a home. Usually, lifetime transfer is only warranted when the real estate is rapidly appreciating and will cause an estate tax greater than the capital gains tax saving resulting from the stepped-up basis.

2. Segmented Gifting. Sometimes it is appropriate to gift over the ownership of a home. If this is done in a single transaction, the value over $10,000 is deducted from the lifetime $600,000 gift and estate tax exclusion. However, by gifting only a portion of the ownership of the real estate each year equal to no more than $10,000 per beneficiary, the additional yearly $10,000 gift exclusion will apply. In this way a $100,000 home could be gifted over a 10-year period and make no dent in the lifetime exclusion.

There are two ways to gift over a house in segments. First, the deed can be changed every year to gift over an increasing fraction of the property equal in value to $10,000. A yearly appraisal of the property with a report that the fractional share transferred equals $10,000 should be made and kept in the file.

Second, under certain circumstances a corporation can be formed to hold the property and shares worth $10,000 transferred each year. This is inappropriate for the transfer of a primary residence, but can work very well for investment and business property.

3. Life Leases and Life Estates. Frequently, a home owner would like to transfer the property but does not want to move out. Transfer can be made and still give lifetime protection to the transferor by creating a life lease or a life estate. In the first case, a lease (which cannot be terminated by the property holder until the death of the lessee) is signed. For example, Dad decides that the best tax strategy is to transfer the home in which he lives and presently owns to his son, but he does not want to move. He wants to protect himself from his son ever evicting him or his daughter-in-law ever claiming occupancy if there is a divorce. This can be accomplished through a deeded transfer with a lifetime lease.

But Dad may think that he will eventually want to move to the Sunbelt. If he does, he would like to rent out the home and generate some income and therefore want to be more than a tenant. A life estate noted on the face of the deed will accomplish this. A life estate gives all the rights of ownership to the life tenant, including renting. But the property cannot be left to anyone other than the son.

Life leases and life estates have created some controversy regarding the estate taxation of the property. If a transferor of the property retains an interest for life in the use of the property, is it completely transferred? Or is there enough control to count the value or a part of it in the transferor's estate? Arguments run high and conclusions are not always consistent. Before you decide on a life estate or life lease, check carefully with a tax attorney or accounting professional for an opinion on the tax consequences for your individual case.

4. Long-Term Health Care and the Home. Perhaps the biggest fear of older people is the possibility of having to sell their homes if they must go into an expensive nursing home for a prolonged period of time. The actual rules vary from state to state, but most allow you to keep your house and still qualify for Medicaid (if you are otherwise qualified) under the following conditions:

- Your spouse still lives there.

- You plan to return someday and have the medical recovery potential to do so.

- You have a dependent child or incompetent adult child who lives there.

- You are joint owner with a sibling who lives there.

Before deciding to transfer a home during your lifetime and give up the stepped-up basis, be sure that there is no other way to protect the home from Medicaid spend-down.

The next most important estate asset for many families is the family business. We will look at those estate aspects in the next Key.

47

BEST PLANNING FOR OWNERS OF A FAMILY BUSINESS

Clearly, the most important estate question facing the family whose income is derived from a family business is, "Will the business survive the proprietor, or will it be sold upon the death of that individual?" Each family must make that decision for itself. In this Key, we will focus on ways to ensure that the decision to save the business for succeeding family members is not thwarted by the estate-tax payments. We will also see the best way to evaluate the family business if it is to be sold in order to minimize the taxes on the estate.

There are two tax rules that help keep the business in the family.

1. *Internal Revenue Code.* If the decedent's estate includes a business whose value exceeds 35 percent or more of the adjusted gross estate, and the corporation has fifteen or fewer shareholders or 20 percent or more of the voting stock of the corporation was owned by the decedent, then payment of much of the tax can be spread over a 15-year period at an interest rate as low as 4 percent.

The purpose of this helpful provision is to allow a family to carry on a business even though high taxes are owed on the estate of the major stockholder. If all taxes were due on death, the family would perhaps have to sell the business to pay them. This rule allows them to make the tax payment as part of the yearly operating expenses.

Many people transfer the value of their shares to other family members before they die (as will be discussed later). This may not be wise, because the 35 percent requirement for payout will not be met. Yet, the value of the shares when transferred is counted in the gross estate.

The value of Section 6166 is not limited to corporate stockholders. A proprietor, a partner (if 20 percent or more of the total capital interest in the partnership is included in the gross estate or there are fifteen or fewer partners), or one having an interest in a holding company that owns the business and is not traded on the stock exchange may also find the rule useful.

2. *IRC 303.* If the value of the stock in the decedent's estate exceeds 35 percent of the gross estate, the corporation can redeem the stock from the estate and have the redemption treated in a tax-favored way.

This 303 redemption rule has been curtailed recently but discuss it with your planner. It may be useful if you have invested heavily in your own business.

Business Evaluation: The final critical step for tax planning and the family business is business evaluation. Section 6166 makes it clear that a high percentage of estate value, if comprised of a family business, can afford a great deal of tax-payout flexibility. On the other hand, it is foolish to inflate the value of a business and therefore increase the tax and pay more just to take advantage of 6166. A business that is not being sold, however, has no definite value so all value judgments are guesses and estimates. The IRS is aware of this fact and accepts several types of evaluation procedures. Many are based on common sense. Here are the most used methods:

multiple of earnings — A business can be evaluated by multiplying the earnings of one year by a factor (often 8 or 10) determined by the type of business. The

IRS accepts rational calculations that can be bolstered by a business broker's independent appraisal.

book value — Usually the lowest valuation, an accountant totes up the assets and subtracts the liabilities to arrive at the value.

contractual value — The shareholders agree what the buy-out value is in the event that one dies or retires. This is only *some* evidence of true value and may be questioned by the IRS.

Minority Share: Once value has been determined, the amount need not be proportional to the amount of shares owned. Minority shareholders may discount the value of their shares under certain circumstances. For example, a one-third owner of a million-dollar company may have shares worth only $200,000 if the minority shares are restricted.

A serious restriction that usually results in a discount is the lack of the right to vote on selling or dissolving the corporation. Less serious restrictions, such as where the corporate headquarters will be, often do not result in discount.

Whether or not we own our own business, we all have a rising expectation of longevity. In the next Key, longevity planning is discussed.

48

MAKE YOUR MEDICAL AND HEALTH CARE WISHES KNOWN

"How do I find a euphemism for death? Let me count the ways." Perhaps that line is not as romantic as a Browning poem, but it is of increasing interest in our long-lived (there's that euphemism again) society. The fact is that we are living longer these days. Some 80 percent of us die in an institution, as opposed to less than 50 percent just a generation ago. This is partially due to prolonged life through artificial means and a legal definition of life itself that would have mystified our ancestors.

Under these circumstances, many people and their advisors work toward controlling even the moment of death. While anything more than a passing nod to this topic is beyond the scope of this book, some of the older readers are quite prepared to deal with the topic. Here are some questions (and answers) of interest to them:

Q. Will my wishes regarding life support devices, medical treatment and other medical procedures really be obeyed?

A. Yes. The days of disallowing the patient the right to dictate medical care are over. In the past, court cases and statutes have resisted such control. Times have changed.

Q. What is the best method for making my wishes known?

A. The best method that I can recommend is to put

instructions in a revocable trust, if you plan to have one, and in a durable power of attorney, which everyone should have (see Key 23).

Q. But I heard about a living will. Isn't that what I should have?

A. You could, but every state has its own rules and regulations regarding the form of such documents, and some are very rigid. Further, they are meant to instruct only your physician, whereas a power will also instruct your fiduciary. A living will works best if given to the treating physician while you are still competent. This is most unlikely, as most people prepare the document while well and therefore without an attending physician. However, you can have both a power and a living will as long as the wishes are absolutely consistent.

Q. What am I permitted to put in the instructions?

A. You can define the level of deterioration that you consider a state of death or nonlife. It must be so severe that the wishes are not suicidal. You can put in a percentage of recovery term, which if you fall below will allow for life-support devices and other treatment to be discontinued. It must be phrased so that the percentage issue doesn't get to court for an interpretation.

You can request to be frozen or to have all possible devices used, regardless of cost.

You can refuse forced feeding, breathing machines, and the like.

You can specify the number of days in a coma before treatment is discontinued.

You can give the discretion to a fiduciary to decide on health care.

Q. This is hard. Are there any forms I can look at?

A. Lots. Your attorney will have many, as will your local department of the aging. Many books are published on death and dying, and several include forms. Societies for the right to die, national councils on death and dying, organizations for concern for the dying—they all have forms. If you cannot locate your local group, call a hospice (facility for the terminally ill) and ask them to direct you to a source.

Q. I'm not married. Can I name my life partner as the decision maker?

A. Yes. Just use the correct forms. The family may interfere, but will most often be preempted if you adhere to the legalities.

Q. You're giving very good information but you're a little tongue-in-cheek. What's bugging you?

A. A very perceptive question. I don't approve of these life-care instructions, but I am told that I am old-fashioned and unrealistic, so I surrender. In my opinion, death is a natural event, as is scientific progress. I see nothing wrong with letting nature take its course, even if part of nature is the use of a machine created by man.

But let's go to the next Key for a discussion of something of which I do approve, choosing an attorney wisely.

49

CHOOSING AN ATTORNEY

While it is never easy to choose a professional, it frequently seems to be particularly difficult to choose a lawyer. They have no board certification and no official specialization. Most shun advertising and don't sign on with referral services. Sounds grim, but don't despair. There are a lot of excellent trusts-and-estates specialists and the ranks are increasing as the field gets more exciting and meaningful to the population at large.

In general, you are looking for a trusts-and-estates specialist, of which there are three categories. A generalist works with estate administration, probate, and drafting all the wills and trusts described in this book. Such a professional is often a member of the state or local bar association committee on trusts and estates or a general practice committee subsection on trusts and estates.

You may be able to get a roster of members from the bar association in your state or county. They may also have a referral service that will provide three names and entitle you to a reduced-rate initial consultation. You might also find a trusts-and-estates attorney through your accountant, financial planner, or insurance agent. Many fee-paid financial planners and commission-based insurance agents will offer a free consultation with a lawyer.

The lawyer gives the free time in exchange for a source of referrals. The planner or agent gives an extra service to the client and therefore gets more business. The client gets a free consultation and (if the lawyer is hired) also a team of professionals who are accustomed to working together and coordinating on cases.

A second type of lawyer is an estate-tax specialist. If your estate is very large and tax-vulnerable, you will need this specialist. That attorney may also do all the drafting and administration but may consult with the generalist on the tax strategies. Many have a special master's degree in tax law and can be found through a law school in your area. They often teach and practice privately.

A third type, growing in popularity, is the eldercare attorney. Such a speciality requires knowledge of the Medicaid/Medicare rules, both state and federal. The backgrounds of these specialists are often governmental, with attorneys most often getting into the field through a state department for the aging or a private aging-advocate, not-for-profit corporation. You will most likely be referred to an elderlaw specialist by your generalist, as you would to a medical specialist by your internist. The referral is usually tried and true. Don't hesitate to use it.

Word of mouth may be the best way to choose a lawyer, but many people have no such help. The public library will have a copy of *Martindale-Hubbell Law Dictionary*, a state-by-state listing of attorneys including address, age, education, and self-proclaimed specialty, among other data.

Martindale-Hubbell also has a rating system based on the opinions of other lawyers in the field. The ratings appear to be a fair indication of competence, but an attorney may ask not to be rated, and some lawyers rate by celebrity status. If I personally needed a lawyer, however, I would check with *Martindale-Hubbell*.

The question of fees is always uppermost in the mind of the public, but cost should not be the most important factor. Considerable researching reveals how similar fees are—even if they don't seem so at first. The higher hourly rate may be charged by a faster lawyer. The flat fee may be increased if the work gets unexpectedly time-consuming.

The best advice is to hire a moderately priced attorney by the hour and cut down the hours with a lot of self-learning. You should know what you want from the estate plan. The client who expects a lawyer to listen to hours of chit-chat about the family and who the beneficiaries are and why the daughter is less favored than the son is going to pay for time that yields no legal-work benefit. Lawyers get impatient and relationships get strained.

Now a final word of advice. If you make the wrong choice, it is cheaper to switch than to remain and be unhappy. In the next Key we will discuss how to choose your accountant.

50

CHOOSING AN
ACCOUNTANT

It will probably be much easier to locate and engage an accountant than it will be to find an attorney for your trusts-and-estates work. There are two reasons for this. First, while many people have an ongoing relationship with an accountant, for personal accounts, income tax, and other reasons, few use an attorney on a regular basis. By all means, if you have an accountant prepare your income tax return, use that one or, if you are an executor or trustee, someone recommended by that individual to prepare an estate-tax return. If you need estate tax planning, try this option first to learn whether these individuals are capable of handling the matter, or perhaps have a recommended referral for you. Second, if you have no source, your lawyer may. Trusts-and-estates lawyers often refer tax preparation or planning work to others. This is particularly true if they are not tax specialists themselves (discussed further in Key 49).

In choosing your accountant, you must make an important distinction between a preparer and a planner. The accountants whom you contact will usually tell you which specialty they practice. The preparer is hired after someone dies to prepare the federal tax Form 706 (see Key 44). The preparer may also do an accounting of the estate, particularly if it is needed for probate. Essentially, this task requires a knowledge of calculation of estate taxes and post-mortem planning (see Keys 26 and 43).

The accountant who is a planner will work with you to project future estate taxes and advise on strategies and clauses that will help reduce the tax. This is also the realm of the tax lawyer—their functions overlap. The one that will do the work depends on the one you consult first. If your estate-tax planner is an accountant, you can use a generalist lawyer to draft the document, but if the tax planner is a lawyer, you can stop shopping.

While many people understand what accountants do quite well, most of them are unaware that there are at least three types of accounting professionals. The most prevalent of the three are public accountants. In many states they need no special licensing. They can prepare returns, including individual, estate, and fiduciary. Some of the major accounting chains hire and train temporary help (especially around tax season) but these chains often do not do estate work, largely because it is not economically feasible for their operations.

A second type of accounting professional is the C.P.A., the certified public accountant. They are state-licensed and require yearly, continuing-education credits to keep that license in most states. They have passed a notoriously difficult test. I have never met an attorney who is also a C.P.A. who has not said that the bar exam was a piece of cake compared with the C.P.A. exam.

Information about C.P.A.s is available from the AICPA, the American Institute of Certified Public Accountants, located at 1211 Avenue of the Americas, New York, NY 10030-8775. The telephone number is (212) 575-6200.

A word from the voice of experience: Many clients have used public accountants found in the Yellow Pages. Some were good—some a disaster. But in most cases, the client believed that the public accountant has

the same background as the C.P.A. Now you know o
erwise.

The third type is a well-kept secret, for no apparent reason. They are enrolled agents. Thcsc professionals have worked as staff in the Internal Revenue Service and are now in private practice. If you find one that was in the IRS estates-and-trusts division, you've made a good choice. This is particularly true if the estate is being audited. Enrollment agents, like the C.P.A., can accompany you to the audit or represent you without your presence. They are usually insiders who often know the ropes. To learn more, contact the National Association of Enrolled Agents, located at 600 Executive Boulevard, Suite 205, Rockwell, MD 20852.

The best advice regarding costs is the same for accounting professionals as for attorneys (see Key 49). Accountant's fees will nearly always be by the hour and somewhat lower than legal fees.

QUESTIONS AND ANSWERS

How important is it to have a will?

Parents of children under the age of 21 and everyone who owns property or investments should definitely have a will. Single people who live with another should also have that protection. In the absence of a will, the court will appoint an administrator at the time of your death, who will distribute your assets according to state law. This distribution may or may not agree with your wishes in the matter.

How important is it to avoid probate?

Whether or not you avoid probate is a matter of individual circumstance. If your heirs have difficulty handling technical matters, you have a complicated estate, or you have property in many states, you should make an effort to avoid probate. If your estate is simple (no matter how large) and you have a trusted accounting or legal professional, probate can be orderly, although it will almost always be more expensive than probate avoidance.

Why can't I just put my money in joint names with right of survivorship, and avoid probate that way?

You can, but that is not recommended because the money is in jeopardy from the creditors and spouse of your joint owner.

So what is the best way to avoid probate?

The best way is to use a revocable trust, also called a living trust. You remain the trustee during your lifetime and handle all the assets. When you die, the successor trustee distributes the assets according to the terms of the trust. The estate never gets to court.

Does the living trust save taxes?

Absolutely not. The taxes on the assets are part of your personal tax return while you are alive. The assets in the trust are part of your gross estate and are taxable or not, depending on normal estate tax rules.

Is there a trust that does save taxes?

Yes. They are irrevocable trusts. You are gifting your money to the trust. The assets belong to the beneficiaries, not to you. Therefore, because you have no control over the money, it is not part of your estate for estate-tax purposes. During your lifetime the trustee files a trust tax return and the trust gets its own tax identification number and bracket.

Can't I keep any control over the assets in an irrevocable trust?

Under limited circumstances, trusts called GRATS, GRITS, and GRUTS allow the grantor (you) to get income only for a limited period of time and still save income and estate taxes.

If I do not have a will, what happens to my estate when I die?

If you have relatives, your property will go to them according to the laws of your state. in the absence of close relatives, it could revert to the state.

What are death taxes? Do they still exist?

Both state and federal governments impose such taxes, but they are called by other names. The federal tax is called an estate tax. States have estate taxes, too, but some states also have inheritance taxes, that is, each beneficiary pays a tax on what is inherited, rather than the estate paying a tax based on its asset value.

At what point is my estate federally taxable?

Everyone has an estate tax exemption of $600,000, and married couples can shield as much as $1,200,000. In addition, you can give money away during your life-time so it is no longer part of your estate.

Suppose I want to disinherit my childen or my spouse. How can I do so?

All states have laws permitting a surviving spouse to inherit a portion of your estate, no matter how you try to avoid it. Your children, though, are a different mat-ter. All you have to do is specify by name in your will that the child or children should receive no part of the estate. In certain states, merely omitting them from one will or trust is enough. An *in-terrorem* clause permits you to declare that a will contest by a disinherited party will result in that person not getting anything.

If I give money away during my lifetime, don't I have to pay a gift tax?

Not necessarily. Every year you can give away $10,000 per person, gift-tax free (married couples $20,000). Further, you can reduce the $600,000 credit if you give more in one year, instead of paying the actual tax.

What is the stepped-up basis, and do I lose it if I give gifts?

The stepped-up basis is a tax rule that applies only if you leave property at death. If you bought real estate or stocks or any other asset at a price lower than its value at date of death, the fiduciary can evaluate it at its higher date-of-death value (basis). In this way, your heirs may pay more in estate tax but far less in capital gains (income) tax if they decided to sell the assets. If you give away the assets during your lifetime, the original basis (your cost plus improvements and the cost of acquisition) follows the gift.

How does the marital deduction work?

Married couples may transfer the ownership of certain assets from one to the other, for the purpose of applying this deduction to one's estate. Both must be U.S. citizens, and only certain kinds of property are eligible for the deduction.

How does a freeze work to reduce estate taxes?

An estate or asset freeze occurs when a family business is reorganized, and all or a portion of the assets are transferred to younger family members. The original owner, however, usually retains an income from the enterprise. At the death of the older family member, the value of the estate for tax purposes is considerably lower than it would have been.

I want to leave a large part of my property to various charities when I die. Is this feasible?

It is not only feasible to make specific contributions to charitable and nonprofit organizations in your will, but it is also frequently done.

How does an executor get appointed?

The person who implements the provisions of your will on your behalf is usually appointed by you. Most often a close relative, your executor should posess some knowledge of your affairs and an understanding of your wishes. Competence and integrity, of course, are also important. If you do not appoint an executor, or if the person you have so designated should die before you, or should become incapacitated, the court will appoint one. For this reason, alternate or successor executors should also be named.

Should I have both a will and a living trust?

Yes. A living trust is a substitute for a will. The trust becomes the owner of all your assets, which are distributed according to your wishes at the time of your death. But if you fail to put all your assets in the name of one trust, there is unnecessary administration. Use a pour-over will to distribute anything still in your name. A pour-over will states that anything not in the trust's name will pour over into the trust at your death.

What is the single best thing I can do to save estate taxes?

The single best thing you can do is to buy the right insurance. A couple can get economical joint and survivor insurance. Proper insurance can be used to pay taxes, create wealth for future generations, and provide liquidity to save a family business or real estate from forced sale. The death benefit can be kept out of the estate and thus be inherited free of tax. An insurance trust can dictate how the proceeds in excess of the taxes are distributed.

GLOSSARY

A

Administrator a person or entity named by the court to represent an estate when there is no will or trust.

Ancillary probate a probate proceeding that takes place in a jurisdiction where the decedent owned property. It is in addition to the proceeding in the jurisdiction where the decedent was domiciled at the time of death.

Annual exclusion the amount that may be excluded from the gift tax. Donors may exclude up to $10,000 per year.

Annuitant the person who establishes and receives the benefits of an annuity.

Annuity an investment usually made through an insurance company that is tax-deferred until withdrawn. It can also be an immediate annuity, which entitles the investor to a specific sum each year for lifetime and/or the lifetime of another under a contractual arrangement with an insurance company.

Attestation clause a clause at the end of a will stating that the witnesses saw the testator sign in their presence, and that they signed in each other's presence and in the testator's presence.

Attorney in fact the person or entity named in the power of attorney to act in the place of the person granting the power.

B

Beneficiary a person or entity entitled to receive trust or estate assets.

Bequest a gift of money or other property under a trust or will.

C

Charitable trust   a trust that benefits the public or a particular class of people, established for charitable, educational, religious, or scientific purposes. Sometimes known as a public trust.

Codicil   an amendment to a will executed with the formalities of a will.

Community property   property acquired by a married couple during the marriage that is deemed to be one-half owned by each. Such property exists in the states of Arizona, New Mexico, Texas, Washington, and (to some extent) Wisconsin.

Conditional gift   a gift that is received or must be returned if a certain event takes place.

Corpus   the Latin term for "body." In the legal sense, corpus refers to the principal of an estate or a bequest. Every trust must have a corpus.

***Crummey* powers**   the right, named after a famous case, to annually withdraw certain amounts from a trust without adverse tax consequences.

Custodian   a person or entity acting as representative of a minor or an incompetent person.

D

Decedent   a legal term referring to a person who has died.

Distributions   the parceling out of estate assets according to the terms of a will or trust.

Domicile   the place where a person permanently resides, which is the jurisdiction where probate takes place.

Durable power of attorney   a power of attorney that remains in effect even when the giver of the power becomes incompetent.

E

Elderlaw   a legal specialty devoted to planning for long-term health care and the rights of incompetent elderly people.

Elective share a state statutory right of a surviving spouse to get a percentage of the decedent spouse's estate, usually one-third, regardless of how much was specified in a will or trust.

Escheat the forfeiture of property to the state where a decedent resided at the time of death.

Estate a body of assets that encompasses all of an individual's real and personal property.

Estate planning the process of determining how to manage and distribute one's property after death, generally at the lowest possible taxation expense.

Estate tax the tax levied upon an individual's net assets following the death of that individual.

Exclusion the amount and types of assets not counted in an estate for tax purposes.

Executor a person or entity named to represent an estate in a will.

F

Fiduciary a person or entity responsible for the custody or management of property, for example, an executor, trustee, or administrator.

Fiduciary duty the high degree of prudence, ethics, and judgment that must be exercised by the fiduciary.

G

Generation-skipping tax the tax that is imposed on generation-skipping trusts. The tax was created because these trusts can avoid the estate or gift tax.

Generation-skipping trust a trust that is established by grandparents to bequeath property to their grandchildren (or great-grandchildren or even younger). The middle generation, although bypassed, sometimes realizes benefits of the property before ownership passes to the next generation(s).

Gift a transfer of ownership from one to another without consideration or compensation.

Gift-tax exclusion the amount of such transfer that can be transferred by law free of tax.

Grantor one making a trust, also called a settlor.

Grantor trust a trust under which the grantor is also the beneficiary of income.

Gross estate the value of all of the property counted in the estate of a decedent, wholly or partially owned by the individual at the time of death, before debts and administrative and funeral expenses have been deducted.

H

Heirs the persons who inherit according to state law, in the absence of a will.

Holographic will a will that is handwritten, dated, and signed. The requirements of witnesses to such a will varies from state to state.

I

Incompetent one who is legally unable to handle one's own affairs, usually caused by a physical or mental disability.

Inheritance tax the state tax imposed on each of the heirs to an estate. The tax rates vary from state to state, and often differ according to the relationship of the heir to the decedent.

In-terrorem a clause in a will or trust stating that those who contest will forfeit their share.

Inter-vivos any trust or provision in a trust that becomes effective during the life of the grantor.

Intestate without a will.

Irrevocable permanent.

Irrevocable trust a trust that cannot be revoked by the grantor.

J

Joint and survivor initial ownership by two persons and then by the survivor of them.

Joint tenancy a shared interest in property by two or more individuals during the lifetime of all. Ownership passes to the survivor(s) at the death of one of the joint tenants.

Joint will one will used as the will for two persons and signed by both. The document is in disfavor with courts and lawyers.

K

Kiddie tax tax structure on the income of a minor.

L

Letter of administration a court-issued document in which person or entity named as administrator of an estate can carry out the prescribed duties.

Letters testamentary a court-ordered document in which a person or entity can carry out the prescribed duties as executor under a will.

Life estate the right to beneficial use, but not ownership, of property for a lifetime.

Life insurance trust a frequent element in estate planning. This kind of trust is the beneficiary of a life-insurance policy

Life lease the right to occupy property for a lifetime.

Living trust a trust that takes effect during the grantor's lifetime.

Living will medical instructions about the use of life-support devices during the illness of the maker.

M

Marital deduction a 100 percent deduction for a gift tax or the amount gifted or left to a spouse from any estate.

N

Net estate the value of all of the property wholly or partially owned by an individual at the time of death, after debts and administrative and funeral expenses have been deducted. The net estate is subject to state and federal taxes.

Noncupative will   an oral will. Such wills are seldom deemed valid, and generally are upheld only when stringent requirements regarding witnesses are observed.

P

Per capita a share given equally to each person.

Per stirpes the circumstance of an inheritance that exists by virtue of the rights of a deceased ancestor.

Post mortem after death, as in "after-death tax planning."

Prenuptial agreement   contract between two people who intend to marry. It outlines the intent of both parties relative to the distribution of the property of each at death or divorce.

Probate a court proceeding to validate a will and carry out the wishes of the testator.

Probate assets   the portion of an estate that is subject to probate and thus becomes a matter of public record.

Pourover will a will that accompanies a living trust and provides that any assets of the decedent that are not held in trust at the time of death pour over into the trust for distribution in accordance with its terms.

Power of attorney a document whereby a person or persons give the right to handle all or part of their assets to another.

Q

QTIP trust a clause in a will that places assets in trust for a spouse upon the death of the other spouse, but still leaves those assets qualified for the unlimited marital deduction. The initials stand for qualified terminable interest property.

R

Renunciation giving up a gift or a bequest, usually for post mortem tax-planning purposes.

Residuary estate whatever is left of an estate after payment of costs, debts, and specific bequests; usually the bulk of an estate.

Revocable a condition that permits amending or revoking at will, for example, "The revocable trust can be revoked by the grantor."

Right of survivorship the right of a joint tenant to take property in its entirety when the other joint owner is deceased.

S

Simultaneous death the death of the testator or grantor and a beneficiary under circumstances in which it cannot be determined who died first.

Spendthrift clause a clause in a will or trust stating that a creditor cannot collect on the future interest of a beneficiary.

Stepped-up basis the circumstance in which the value of a beneficiary's bequest is increased to the level of its value at the time of the decedent's date of death (or six months later).

Successor one named in a will or trust to replace a trustee or executor who cannot serve.

Surrogate a judge of the surrogate court who is charged with acting according to the wishes of the decedent.

T

Taxable estate that part of the gross estate that is subject to federal taxes, generally after marital and charitable deductions have been applied.

Tenants-in-common two or more parties who own property jointly, but without right of survivorship, that is, when one dies, heirs will inherit the share of the decedent.

Tenants by the entirety ownership by husband and wife.

Testamentary any provision found in a will or that takes effect at death.

Testator one making a will.

Totten trust a bank account that is payable to a named beneficiary upon the death of the depositor. The trust is revocable and is used in place of a will.

Trust a document transferring assets from one party to another for the benefit of a third.

Trustee the person or entity named to act as the fiduciary of the trust and to whom the grantor transfers property for the benefit of another.

U

Unified credit a tax credit by the federal government that is applied to either estate or gift taxes.

Uniform Gifts to Minors Act law that has been adopted by all fifty states, which permits an adult to make a monetary gift in trust to a minor.

W

Will a document leaving the assets of the decedent to named beneficiaries.

Will contest a challenge to a will, often initiated by disgruntled family members. The will in question has usually been made just prior to the death of the maker.

ADDITIONAL REFERENCES

American Bar Association, Real Property, Probate and Trust Law Section Staff, *Post-Mortem Tax Planning and Problems After ERTA: The Complete Picture.* Chicago: American Bar Association. 1982, 356 pp, $25.

Berg, Adriane G., *Making up for Lost Time: Speed Investing for a Secure Future*, New York, Hearst, 1994.

Boroson, Warren, *Keys to Retirement Planning.* Hauppauge, NY: Barron's Educational Series, Inc. 1990, 160 pp, $4.95 (Canada $6.50).

Crumbley, Lawrence and Edward E. Milam, *Keys to Estate Planning and Trusts.* Hauppauge, NY: Barron's Educational Series, Inc. 1989, 160 pp, $4.95 (Canada $6.50).

Gifis, Steven H., *Dictionary of Legal Terms.* Hauppauge, NY: Barron's Educational Series, Inc. 1983, 511 pp, $7.95 (Canada $10.95).

_____ , *Law Dictionary,* 3rd edition. Hauppauge, NY: Barron's Educational Series, Inc. 1991, 537 pp, $11.95 (Canada $15.95).

Hansen, Leonard J., *Life Begins at 50.* Hauppauge, NY: Barron's Educational Series, Inc. 1989, 250 pp, $11.95 (Canada $15.95).

Jurinsky, James J., *Keys to Preparing a Will*. Hauppauge, NY: Barron's Educational Series, Inc. 1991, 140 pp, $5.95 (Canada $6.95).

National Business Institute Staff, *Probate and Tax Administration of the Estate*. Eau Claire, Wis.: National Business Institute. 1987, $30.

_____, *Probate: Beyond the Basics*. Eau Claire, Wis.: National Business Institute. 1987, $30.

Saltman, David and Harry Schaffner, *Don't Get Married Until You Read This*. Hauppauge, NY: Barron's Educational Series, Inc. 1989, 202 pp, $9.95 (Canada $13.95).

Yogis, John, *Law Dictionary, Canadian*, 2nd edition. Hauppauge, NY: Barron's Educational Series, Inc. 1990, 288 pp, $13.95.

INDEX

BARRON'S BUSINESS KEYS Each "key" explains approximately 50 concepts and provides a glossary and index. Each book: Paperback, approx. 160 pp., 4³⁄₁₆" x 7", $4.95, Can. $6.50.

Keys for Women Starting or Owning a Business (4609-9)
Keys to Avoiding Probate and Reducing Estate Taxes (4668-4)
Keys to Business and Personal Financial Statements (4622-6)
Keys to Buying a Foreclosed Home (4765-6)
Keys to Buying a Franchise (4484-3)
Keys to Buying and Owning a Home, 2nd Edition (9032-2)
Keys to Buying and Selling a Business (4430-4)
Keys to Choosing a Financial Specialist (4545-9)
Keys to Conservative Investments, 2nd Edition (9006-3)
Keys to Estate Planning and Trusts, 2nd Edition (1710-2)
Keys to Financing a College Education, 2nd Edition (1634-3)
Keys to Improving Your Return on Investments (ROI) (4641-2)
Keys to Incorporating, 2nd Edition (9055-1)
Keys to Investing in Common Stocks, 2nd Edition (9004-7)
Keys to Investing in Corporate Bonds (4386-3)
Keys to Investing in Government Securities, 2nd Edition (9150-7)
Keys to Investing in International Stocks (4759-1)
Keys to Investing in Municipal Bonds (9515-4)
Keys to Investing in Mutual Funds, 3rd Edition (9644-4)
Keys to Investing in Options and Futures, 2nd Edition (9005-5)
Keys to Investing in Real Estate, 2nd Edition (1435-9)
Keys to Investing in Your 401(K) (1873-7)
Keys to Managing Your Cash Flow (4755-9)
Keys to Mortgage Financing and Refinancing, 2nd Edition (1436-7)
Keys to Personal Financial Planning, 2nd Edition (1919-9)
Keys to Personal Insurance (4922-5)
Keys to Purchasing a Condo or a Co-op (4218-2)
Keys to Reading an Annual Report, 2nd Edition (9240-6)
Keys to Retirement Planning, 2nd Edition (9013-6)
Keys to Risks and Rewards of Penny Stocks (4300-6)
Keys to Saving Money on Income Taxes, 2nd Edition (9012-8)
Keys to Starting a Small Business (4487-8)
Keys to Starting an Export Business (9600-2)
Keys to Surviving a Tax Audit (4513-0)
Keys to Understanding Bankruptcy, 2nd Edition (1817-6)
Keys to Understanding the Financial News, 2nd Edition (1694-7)
Keys to Understanding Securities (4229-8)
Keys to Women's Basic Professional Needs (4608-0)

Barron's Educational Series, Inc.
250 Wireless Boulevard • Hauppauge, NY 11788
In Canada: Georgetown Book Warehouse
34 Armstrong Avenue, Georgetown, Ont. L7G 4R9

(#10) R 6/97